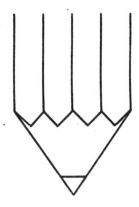

**Classroom Practices
in Teaching English
1975-1976**

On Righting Writing

D1127947

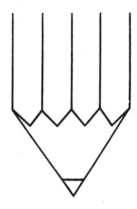

Classroom Practices
in Teaching English
1975-1976

On Righting Writing

Thirteenth Report
of the Committee
on Classroom Practices
Ouida H. Clapp, Chair
National Council of Teachers of English
1111 Kenyon Road, Urbana, Illinois 61801

NCTE COMMITTEE ON CLASSROOM PRACTICES IN TEACHING
ENGLISH: Ouida H. Clapp, Buffalo Board of Education, New York, Chair;
Jeffrey N. Golub, Kent Junior High School, Washington; Norman Nathan,
Florida Atlantic University; Sandra Y. Seale, McClymonds High School,
Oakland, California; Gene Stanford, Utica College of Syracuse University;
Robert E. Beck, *ex officio*, John Swett High School, Crockett, California; Allen
Berger, University of Pittsburgh, consultant.

NCTE EDITORIAL BOARD: Charles R. Cooper, Evelyn M. Copeland,
Bernice E. Cullinan, Richard Lloyd-Jones, Frank Zidonis, Robert F. Hogan,
ex officio, Paul O'Dea, *ex officio*. STAFF EDITOR: Carol Schanche. BOOK
DESIGN: Rob Carter.

NCTE Stock Number: 06854

Library of Congress Cataloging in Publication Data

National Council of Teachers of English. Committee on
    Classroom Practices.
    ·On righting writing.

    (Classroom practices in teaching English; 1975-1976)
    Includes bibliographical references.
    1. English language—Composition and exercises.
I. Clapp, Ouida H.   II. Title.   III. Series.
LB1631.N3   1975   808'.042   75-26121
ISBN 0-8141-0685-4

Contents

v

Sharpening Technique

Writing to Clarify Values

Exploring Writing Systems

Preface

Participants in the open meeting of the Committee on Classroom Practices in Teaching English at the Sixty-Fourth Annual Convention of the National Council of Teachers of English in New Orleans, November, 1974, expressed great concern for the quality of student writing. There was no doubt in the mind of anyone attending the meeting that the improvement of writing instruction should be the theme of this issue of *Classroom Practices in Teaching English.*

Invitations for manuscripts were placed in the March, 1974 issues of *Elementary English, English Journal* and *College English* as well as in newsletters and journals of many NCTE affiliates. In addition, editors of various interested subject-related journals cooperated in publishing notices requesting manuscripts.

Committee members Jeffrey Golub, Norman Nathan, Sandra Seale, Gene Stanford, and the committee chairman read and evaluated a total of 148 manuscripts which were submitted by elementary, secondary, college and university teachers, English chairmen, and program supervisors and coordinators from thirty-six states, Canada, England, and the Virgin Islands. Manuscripts selected from these 148 were read by each member of the NCTE Editorial Board.

Although a practice described by a writer may have been used at a particular grade level, in many instances that practice will be applicable for some use by the reader at all levels of instruction.

The committee appreciates the wide interest shown in the publication and hopes that *On Righting Writing* will be of real assistance to the many teachers who look forward to the annual publication of *Classroom Practices.*

Getting the Writer Started

Why Not Try a Writer's Corner?

Eileen Tway

Preparing a retreat that motivates children to write is described by Eileen Tway, sixth grade teacher at McGuffey School, Miami University, Oxford, Ohio.

Modern classrooms usually have one or more interest centers or corners, such as a reading nook or a science table. Not so usual, though, is a corner for writing. Yet today's children ought to have a quiet place to retreat for personal writing as well as a place for reading comfort. A portable screen can be set up with an appropriate sign to show that it marks the Writing Corner, and another important interest center is available in the classroom. Behind the screen can be a table, chairs, all kinds of paper, all kinds of writing tools, and a shoe box full of inviting ideas. Here children can come when they would like to create, to record feelings, or to experiment with words. The Writer's Corner should be a stimulant to ongoing writing experiences in the classroom.

In my own sixth-grade classroom the children use our Writer's Corner more for a retreat for either personal or team writing than for ideas. The children have their own ideas and need only time and place — along with some teacher guidance — to develop them. Still, there are story starters and idea booklets available in the corner for those who need a little inspiration. From time to time books written by children are displayed; they can be books the children in the school or neighboring schools have produced by hand or they can be commercial books which are written by children or which contain children's writings. Books and stories that other children have written can provide inspiration for children to try to write their own material.

Young children or children who have not developed the inner motivation for writing may need more stimulators in the Writer's Corner. The presence of different kinds of writing tools and different kinds and colors of paper is important. Research shows that children are more creative when they can choose the materials and tools that suit them best. According to Krzesni (1971),[1] freedom to choose a ballpoint pen, colored pen, or different size

---

[1] Joseph S. Krzesni, "Effect of Different Writing Tools and Paper on Performance of the Third Grader," *Elementary English*, 48 (November 1964), 821-824.

2

pencil seemed to lead to better writing results. Other stimulators include a small file box with one-sentence story starters on cards, a larger file box with amusing or strange pictures, and a shoe box with story ideas clipped from children's magazines. The stimulators should be changed or varied rather often to keep the Writer's Corner from going stale. Other possibilities are the commercial kits or author booklets that are appearing on the market.

Stimulation outside the Writer's Corner is still important. The life of the classroom should be enriched with children's literature. Richard Adams of *Watership Down* fame says that nobody can write who does not read a great deal.[2] The Writer's Corner fosters the inner stimulation that grows from the outside encouragement. If educators value writing, then the classroom environment should be stimulating for writing as well as for other activities. If the classroom is not large enough for another corner, then the interest corners could be alternated monthly or at other intervals.

The Writer's Corner is another means to get away from the practice of every child doing the same thing at the same time, such as in whole-class writing assignments. Whole-class assignments or choices may have their place, but surely not for every writing experience. Why not encourage children to do personal writing in their free time, choice time, or study time? Why not try a Writer's Corner?

Selected Books Containing Children's Writings

Adoff, Arnold, ed. *It Is the Poem Singing into Your Eyes: Anthology of New Young Poets.* New York: Harper and Row, 1971. Adoff has brought together a discriminating selection of poems.

Baron, Virginia Olson, ed. *Here I Am!: An Anthology of Poems Written by Young People in Some of America's Minority Groups.* New York: Dutton.

Conkling, Hilda. *Poems by a Little Girl.* Philadelphia: Stokes, 1920. Hilda Conkling was ten years old when her poems were published.

Dunning, Stephen, ed. *Mad, Sad, and Glad.* New York: Scholastic, 1970. Poems from Scholastic Creative Writing Awards.

Jordan, June, and Terri Bush, eds. *The Voice of the Children.* New York: Holt, Rinehart, and Winston, 1970. Verse is from a creative writing workshop.

Joseph, Stephen H., ed. *The Me Nobody Knows: Children's Voices from the Ghetto.* New York: Avon (paperback), 1972. This is a collection of prose and poetry by New York City youngsters.

Larrick, Nancy, ed. *Green Is Like a Meadow of Grass.* New York: Garrard, 1968. The poems are by children whose teachers were participants in a poetry workshop.

---

[2] Richard Adams, Annual Banquet Address, NCTE Convention, New Orleans, November 30, 1974.

Larrick, Nancy, ed. *I Heard a Scream in the Street: Poetry by Young People in the City.* New York: Evans, 1970.

Lewis, Richard, ed. *Miracles: Poems by Children of the English-Speaking World.* New York: Simon and Schuster, 1966.

Lewis, Richard, ed. *Journeys: Prose by Children of the English-Speaking World,* 1969.

Straight, Dorothy. *How the World Began.* New York: Pantheon, 1964. Dorothy was four when she told and illustrated her story of how the world began.

Sustained Silent Silence

George S. Lamb and John C. Towner
Western Washington State College

One technique which capitalizes on children's communicative needs is Sustained Silent Silence. This technique is designed to supplement existing writing and reading programs. Unlike other techniques, Sustained Silent Silence requires that writing be the only medium of communication. The trick is to create or recognize situations in which children *must* communicate with one another as well as the teacher.

This technique has been used successfully in a variety of situations. One sixth-grade teacher reaped unexpected benefits from a silent math period. Students wrote their names on the board if they needed help, and communicated with the teacher and other classmates in writing. By the time help came, many had figured the problems out for themselves! They also learned the value of skipping ahead and returning to a troublesome problem, something the teacher had been unable to accomplish previously.

One child, who was being tutored in reading, benefitted from written communication with his tutor. It was discovered through his fluent written responses that he had easily read the tutor's written notes. His problem was not a skill deficit so much as an expectancy set about how he thought he was supposed to read a book.

At the present time, we have some theoretical bases and some limited experience to support the idea that Sustained Silent Silence should help children to think, to write, and to read. We do not suggest that it be used as a major program in any way; we do suggest that it be tried as a supplementary technique to encourage children's writing. We are anxious to learn more about it ourselves, and would appreciate receiving descriptions from teachers who try it.

Needed: Stimulus for a Story

Elinor P. Ross

Three productive avenues to the stimulus children need for writing stories are described by Elinor P. Ross, assistant professor at Tennessee Technological University, Cookeville, Tennessee.

Children cannot be expected to write creatively in a vacuum. Given no more than a blank sheet of paper and a time limit, few children can create stories. They need inspiration. Many commercially prepared creative writing kits provide children with titles and opening lines to get them started. The following suggestions may also be useful in helping children begin to write. The three categories are designed to elicit three different types of creative writing.

Reactions and Reflections

By encouraging children to react to and reflect upon their experiences, teachers can make them more sensitive to their environment and more aware of their feelings. Such writing can offer an emotional release by letting children express indirectly what has been troubling them or making them happy.

Sociodramatic Situations. Children are presented with situations resembling those which they encounter in their daily lives. These situations may cause students to make decisions and judgments involving values, ethics, and morals. Such writing may have a therapeutic value by allowing children to explore their feelings and understand different points of view.

Response to Pictures. Provide some pictures representing situations in which conflict exists. Discuss them briefly, and encourage the children to select one with special meaning for them. Then let them imagine a dramatic scene in which they write their impression of the conflict and how it is resolved.

Music for Mood. Different kinds of music provoke different reactions. Before playing any music, ask the children to close their eyes while they listen to what the music seems to be saying and think how it makes them feel. Then play a moving classical selection, such as *The William Tell Overture* or *The 1812 Overture.* Give them the opportunity to write their interpretation of what they have heard.

5

Cloud Pictures. On a day when white cumulus clouds are drifting in a blue sky, take the children outside and give them time to dream. Encourage them to imagine what they see in the cloud shapes. As the clouds float, merge, and change their shapes, the children can develop their story lines. Bring them inside while the images are still fresh and give them time to write their reactions.

Color Cues. Show and discuss paintings that reveal the brilliance and subtleties of colors, or read poetry about colors from *Hailstones and Halibut Bones* (O'Neill).[1] Give the children time to think of what colors mean to them or do for them. Then encourage them to select a color that evokes mental images, moods, or special associations. Ask them to respond to the colors they have chosen in words that reflect their own emotions and experiences.

Sights and Sounds. Take the children outside to listen to the sounds around them and to see the movement of people and things. As they listen and watch, let them write words and phrases describing these sights and sounds. Help them see the possibilities for rhythm and alliteration as they group their words and phrases to form prose or poetry.

Sensory Impressions. Discuss the five senses and help the children see that they need all of their senses in order to fully perceive their environment. Encourage them to choose a topic, such as spring or the first snowfall. Ask them how they can see, smell, hear, taste, and touch spring. Let them use descriptive words that form vivid sensory images.

Structured Stories

Children can understand the elements and structure of stories by patterning their own stories from existing forms. As they analyze the stories they read, they begin to recognize certain features which are repeated.

Original "Just So" Stories. Rudyard Kipling's wonderful stories of "How the Camel Got His Hump" and "How the Leopard Got His Spots" can provide inspiration for the children's own "How" stories. Let them select animals with distinctive physical features and supply their own reasons for their existence. For instance, they can write "How the Turtle Got His Shell" or "How the Pelican Got His Bill."

Fairy Tales. Fairy tales are models of direct storytelling with clearly defined characters and swift-moving plots. Children can select one of the popular motifs, such as enchanted people or magical objects. Then they can construct their own fairy tales based on these familiar fairy tale patterns.

---

1 Mary O'Neill. *Hailstones and Halibut Bones* (Garden City, New York: Doubleday and Company, 1961).

The Fable Formula. Children can read or listen to many different fables until they can identify the characteristics. They might begin writing their own fable by thinking of a moral. Then they could choose animal characters to illustrate this moral in a brief episode.

Updated Nursery Rhymes. At a very young age children become acquainted with nursery rhymes, and throughout their lives they will hear allusions to them. By combining familiar tales with some imagination, the children can create fresh versions of nursery rhymes by placing them in modern settings. For instance, what would happen today if Mary's lamb followed her to a new open-space schoolhouse?

Story Endings. Some stories create a great deal of suspense and end with a surprise. Read the children this type of story and stop at the climax. Let them write their own endings and then compare them with the original version.

Dealing the Cards. Rather than following an existing model, children can take elements of a story and write a version of what might happen. Cards containing story parts could be dealt to the children or selected by them. The children would get three character cards, such as a villian, an old man, and a small child; a setting card telling the time and place; a plot card briefly stating the beginning of a story line; and a conflict card which would furnish the action. These essential elements can be used as the framework for a story.

Let's Pretend

With a little encouragement, children release their imaginations and creative impulses in their writing. All that many of them need is the opportunity to put their dreams and wishes on paper. This type of writing encourages divergent thinking and creative solutions to problems.

"What if" Situations. Provide the children with a list of imaginative situations beginning with "What if ...." Ask them to think about one of these situations and to stretch their imaginations as they write their responses. Examples would be: "What if I had three legs?" "What if everyone looked alike?" "What would happen if there were no gravity?"

A Make-Believe World. Many children enjoy fantasy. They like to escape to a world inhabited by dragons, giants, elves, monsters, and fairy princesses. Encourage them to let their imaginations run free so that they can create a story in which they become part of this make-believe world. They can satisfy their egos by making themselves heroes or wise and fair rulers, or they can turn magically into anything they wish to be.

Nonsense Stories. Let the children draw cards on which are written phrases such as "swollen snout," "battered jalopy," "pink and green striped zebra," "leaping skeletons," and "spooky sirens." From these phrases, encourage them to write the silliest, most ridiculous tales they can imagine.

Three Magic Wishes. Every child has secret wishes which often reveal inner feelings. Let the child suppose that a magician granted him or her three wishes. What would the wishes be? What would the consequences be?

Another Era. Children might like to imagine what it would be like for a famous person to live during another period in history or at a time in the future. For instance, what would Thomas Edison think if he saw the many ways lights are used today? How would Columbus feel if he revisited America in the twentieth century?

The Other Road. Robert Frost wrote of two roads that diverged in a wood and said that he took the one less traveled by.[2] Ask the children to think of a time in their lives when they choose one of two or more alternatives. Let them imagine what would be happening to them now if they had taken the other road.

Story Starters. Provide the students with a selection of titles or first lines for stories. These may be taken from commercial materials or teacher prepared lists. An idea for a title might be "The Night the Moon Fell from the Sky." A first line might be, "We first heard the mysterious moaning when we were exploring the old cave one Saturday morning."

Within each child lie hidden stories. By providing the stimuli, the teacher uncovers these stories and releases creative activity.

[2] Robert Frost. *The Road Not Taken* (New York: Holt, Rinehart and Winston, 1967), 270–71.

I Can Say It, but I Can't Write It Down

Jacqueline Griffin
Essex County College
Newark, New Jersey

Here we are, fellow composition teachers, in one of the most verbal cultures in the world, surrounded by students who tell us, "I have nothing to say," or more frequently, "I can't put it down in words." These same students can talk our ears off because they have been surrounded with words since birth. Current research shows that cultural minorities, contrary to "popular" belief, are highly verbal in their own environments. Furthermore, most children in America are bombarded with words on radio and television. What the student is really saying to us is "I can't put it in writing because I don't know that kind of English."

Twenty-Eight Creative Ideas for Writing

Ronald L. Cramer

Teachers of beginning writers used a series of ideas to spark their students' imagination. Ronald L. Cramer is professor at Oakland University, Rochester, Michigan, and presently visiting professor at St. John's College, York University, York, England.

The ideas in this article were contributed by practicing teachers who were especially interested in creative writing. They have all been tried and proved useful in the classroom. Each idea contains the nucleus of a writing concept and some information about how to implement the idea. Some are directed to the teacher, others to the students.

Ideas for Beginning Writing

1. Before show-and-tell or sharing time, encourage children to write two or three sentences about what they are going to share. This activity may help the child to organize thoughts for a more effective presentation, but should be used only occasionally.

2. Read "What Is Big" from *Sounds of Numbers* by Bill Martin, Jr., and Peggy Brogan (Holt, Rinehart and Winston, 1972). Talk about things that are bigger and smaller than the children. Pass out diagonally cut paper. Children who wish to draw themselves as the biggest object begin at the large end of the paper. Example: a boy, a sled, a pan, a tomato, a bug. Children who wish to draw themselves small begin at the small end of the paper. Example: a girl, a stove, a car, a tree, a house. Have the children write the name of each object above it.

3. Cut out pictures from magazines and make a collage with a theme, such as happy, angry, excited, sad, lazy, brave, sleepy, cold, hungry, and so on. Label the collage with the one word that best describes it.

4. Staple thirteen pages of paper together with a cover. Beginning with the letter "A," label each page with a letter of the alphabet. As children learn new words from their writing activities, the teacher can help them write the words in their dictionaries.

Ideas for Beginning Writing

5. Choose the opening sentence of a short story or play and discuss all the information the reader is given in that one sentence. When the activity

9

is completed, children should practice writing their own opening sentences. Here is an example from Chekov's *The Lady with the Dog*: "It was reported that a new face had been seen on the quay; a lady with a little dog." Information given: setting is a port, seaside resort, or fishing village; gossip circulated about the new person in town; somebody finds this new person newsworthy; the new person has a dog.

6. Many things happen in the classroom that are worth writing about. When an interesting event occurs, discuss the sequence of events that preceded the event and what occurred afterward. List these on the board. Then have the class construct a story about the incident.

7. A good title is usually brief and striking in its effect on the reader. It often sums up the essence of the picture or story or gives a clue to content or meaning. Try inventing some titles that meet these criteria. Display several large pictures in front of the class. After study and discussion of the pictures, encourage the children to write titles for each picture. In some cases single words will be best and in other instances phrases may be appropriate. For children who have difficulty with this activity, try getting them to write brief sentences about each picture. Then work on reducing the sentences to a word or phrase.

8. Read a story where several endings are plausible. Sometimes this activity requires modifying the original ending or leaving it off. Have the children suggest possible alternative endings and their consequences. Then ask them to write their own endings to the story. Jack London, Edgar Allan Poe, and O. Henry have written many short stories that are particularly useful for this type of activity.

Ideas for Creative Thinking

9. Make a list of things you would like to do before you die. Think seriously about it and be sincere. A man once made a list of one hundred things he wanted to do, and by the time he was forty years old he had done all but five of them. Look in travel magazines and consult reference books to help you visualize some possibilities.

10. Here are some questions that may be used as ideas for writing:

What is the quietest sound you know?
What is the nosiest racket you've ever heard?
If you could meet a special person who is not alive today, whom would you choose?
What would you say in a note that was going to be put in a bottle and cast into the sea?
If you could choose ten things to put in a time capsule to be opened in 100 years, what items would you select?
If you were stranded on a deserted island, what ten things would you want to have along with you?

11. Here are some "what if . . ." situations. Choose one of them and write about it. If you prefer, you can make up your own "what if . . . ."

What if you were principal of your school?
What if there were no cars?
What if you had one hundred dollars to spend?
What if you had no legs?
What if you owned a large ranch?
What if you had your own yacht?
What if the president of the United States asked you to be ambassador to India?
What if . . .

12. Pretend you belong to a "Liar's Club." There is a contest with prizes to be awarded for the "biggest whopper" of the year. Here are some topics around which you may write a championship "whopper": sports, hobbies, heroic deeds, pets, family, where you live, friends.

Ideas on Feelings and Values

13. Pretend you are on a life raft and are the only survivor of a shipwreck. Tell how you would survive and the different feelings you might have during your ordeal at sea.

14. Think of all the words that you associate with a word like *loneliness*. Write these words in a box in the corner of a paper. Try to use these words in a story or a poem about *loneliness*.

15. Have you ever wished you could change the world? When things don't go the way we had hoped, we often wish we could. Imagine that you have the power to change things the way you'd like them to be. What things would you change? What things would remain the same? How would you feel about these changes?

16. When you watch the news on TV or read the newspapers, it sometimes seems that certain things need to be changed or improved in our country, state, or city. If you could make five changes in your country, state, or city, what would they be? Why?

Ideas for Writing Poetry

17. Read poetry to children. From this activity other ideas may occur to you. For example, as you read you may occasionally stop and ask them to supply the next line. Everything in poetry starts from listening to it and enjoying the experience.

18. Read the poem "Elegy for Job" by John Ciardi. When people die, they sometimes have an epitaph written on their gravestone. Often epitaphs are serious, but sometimes they are humorous. In Boot Hill, a graveyard for outlaws and cowboys, one epitaph reads simply, "He called Bill Jones a

Liar." Try writing an epitaph for the following people: a cowboy who died in a gunfight, an old lady who loved animals, a soldier killed in war, a faithful country doctor, a famous singer, a corrupt politician, a policeman killed on duty.

19. Write a poem about the way things are but should not be. A poem like this says things one way but means them another way. Sometimes this is called *irony* or *satire*. Here is a poem that says things one way but means them another:

> Lovely, acrid, billowing factory smoke
> Obscures the ugliness of distant snowcapped mountains
> Trucks rumble quietly over the thruways depositing lovely black soot
> On corroded picturesque city slums
> Children chatter happily on their way to school
> Coughing, laughing, rubbing their eyes in delight
> As the city gasps gaily to life.

20. Write acrostic poems where the first letter in each line can be read vertically to form a word. Here is an acrostic poem:

> The snow falls solemnly
> Obscuring the bare fields
> It glides gently in the air
> Like dandelions gone to seed

The vertical word is *toil*, which means to work.

21. Write a concrete or picture poem. Concrete poetry expresses an idea in both verbal and pictorial form. It's fun, easy, and you'll like the things you can do with it.

```
               jj
              jinj
             jinglj
            jinglebj
           jinglebelj
          jinglebelljj
         jinglebelljinj
        jinglebelljinglj
       jinglebelljinglebj
      jinglebelljinglebelj
     jinglebelljinglebelljj
    jinglebelljinglebelljinj
   jinglebelljinglebelljinglj
  wewishyouamerrychristmaswe
```

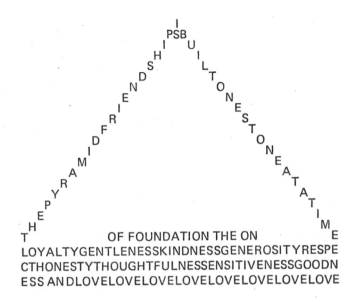

Ideas for Story Writing

22. Read a story which requires the solving of a code as part of the plot, such as *Tony's Treasure Hunt* by Holly and John Peterson (Franklin Watts Publishing Inc., New York). Write a story which has a code as part of the plot. *The First Book of Codes and Ciphers* by Sam and Beryl Epstein (Franklin Watts Publishing Inc., 1956) will teach you how to write codes.

23. You are on a spaceship traveling to another galaxy. You were born on the ship and now are ten years old. Describe a day in your life from the time you get up until the time you go to bed. Remember to include such things as the clothing you wear, the food you eat, the education you receive, and how you entertain yourself.

24. Read *Have You Seen My Brother* by Elizabeth Guilfoile (Follett Publishing Co., 1962). Many young children have been lost and this book will encourage them to express their feelings and emotions about this common experience.

Ideas for Editing

25. Two editing charts can be placed in the writing center to help children edit their own materials. One chart has some reminders about the mechanics of writing, and the other chart contains reminders about content and meaning.

Content Chart:

Did I say what I wanted to say clearly?
Did I say it so that others will understand?
Did I arrange the paragraphs in a logical and interesting way?
Did I use the best possible words throughout my writing?
Did my story have a good beginning, middle, and ending?
Did I make the people and events in my story seem real, interesting,
    and worth reading about?

Mechanics Chart:

Did I punctuate each sentence?
Did I use punctuation in other appropriate places?
Did I capitalize the first word of each sentence?
Did I capitalize other appropriate words?
Did I spell each word correctly or check on the spelling of words I
    was unsure about?
Did I use proper form on titles, margins, indenting, and other matters?
Did I write in my best handwriting?

26. If you have written a story or a play, it is sometimes helpful to have it acted out by others while you watch. If you listen carefully, you may discover that the story or play needs some rewriting to improve it.

27. Read your story or account, and write some questions about the most important things in it. Ask a partner to read it, then see if your partner can answer your questions. If your partner has trouble, either ask someone else to read it for a second opinion, or rewrite your story to be sure that it is written clearly and is well organized.

28. Make arrangements with a class of fifth or sixth grade children to work with your younger children. On specified occasions they may serve as editors. Young children will often react more positively to older children than to an adult. When this activity is done, care must be taken to instruct the older children both in the techniques of editing as well as in the techniques of working gently with younger authors.

Conclusion

Writing is a way of communicating with ourselves, of splashing our personality in ink stains upon the printed page, of discovering inner feelings. Children are able to articulate and clarify their inner feelings and thoughts through writing. Writing can be joyful! It can open new horizons to the minds and imaginations of children.

Treasure Hunt

Chad Lincoln
Carmel Middle School
Carmel, California

The "treasure hunt" is an easily adaptable means of combatting "classtrophobia" while providing valuable learning experiences. This variation involves the notion of metaphor and simile, so important to the understanding of poetry and prose. Students working singly or in pairs are given lists of metaphors and similes ("crazy descriptions") and told to find each item, all of which can be found in the classroom; then they must write their own descriptive phrase for each. They are warned not to skip any because each item contains a clue to the next. The list could be supplemented with items specific to a particular classroom.

1. The ogre's throne
2. The dragon's tail
3. Like a petrified snake
4. As a turbine that needs oil
5. The talking eye
6. A coffee pot
7. Like a "Hello"
8. Colorful fireworks
9. Like an escape hatch
10. Like an oink
11. A memory of summer
12. Holding many voices
13. The ice bucket
14. Like the sky
15. Like a sandy beach

1. Teacher's chair. Tag reads: Go to the board and write "Ever see one?" Then skip number 2. 3. Window opener. Tag reads: Go on to number 4. 4. Pencil sharpener. Tag reads: Go on to number 5. 5. The clock. Tag reads: On the available scratch paper write "If you smile, I'll smile" and hand it to the nearest person. If he or she smiles, smile back; if *not*, stick out your tongue. In any event, skip numbers 6 and 7. 8. The U.S. flag. Tag reads: Go to number 9. 9. The door. Tag reads: Go to number 10. 10. The wastebasket. Tag reads: Skip number 11; go on to number 12. 12. The book shelf. Tag reads: Go up to the teacher and say "Lemons"; if the teacher fails to say "Forget the ice bucket" say "I'm going on to number 14" and do so. 14. The ceiling. Tag reads: Go to number 15. 15. The blackboard. Tag reads: Go to the blackboard and write "That's it!"; then go to the teacher, turn in your own "crazy descriptions" of these and smile. You've done it!

Young Authors Conference

Bessie Baker

Students from nine schools gave each other tips on writing at a conference for young writers. Bessie Baker, coordinator of resource teachers in Nampa, Idaho, School District #31, tells about the project.

Was there a potential Jack London, or an Emily Dickinson, or perhaps an Ogden Nash in the group of young authors assembled at South Junior High School, Nampa, Idaho, March 14, 1975, attending the fifth annual Young Authors Conference? Could very well be!

According to resource teachers from the nine participating elementary schools, 120 young authors attended. Children from grades one through six participate in a creative writing project each spring, preparing books and stories to share with their classmates and with their families.

Each school has its own way of motivating students to write stories. One elementary school has a little house, "casita," constructed in one corner of the classroom; the first floor of the casita offers a private place where a child may go with a tape recorder and be undisturbed as he or she creates a story. The second floor, reached by a ladder fastened to the wall, resembles a penthouse, and it also offers privacy for the student composing a story, or perhaps two students quietly enjoying a chess game after completing creative writing activities.

In another school, a brightly colored bathtub called "Chitty-Chitty Bang Bang" by third-grade children furnishes a "fun-place" for children to use as a quiet place for reading, or for creative writing without intrusion.

In still another classroom, a miniature "castle on the Rhine" provides a retreat for a first grade author who can dictate a "book" to an easily operated tape recorder. Then, a volunteer senior citizen transcribes the story, and the student is "in print."

These are only techniques to give children a sense of privacy as they compose creatively. A child who might sit at a desk and stare at a blank sheet of paper, often will work enthusiastically and well if alone in a small enclosure.

After the children have written their "books," the teacher selects the five best stories and gives them to the resource teacher. Resource teachers then determine a winner from among the five. That child is then invited to attend

16

the Conference. If stories are illustrated by someone other than the author, that person, too, attends the Conference, explained Mrs. Erva Verner, Title I coordinator.

During the Conference, the young authors meet in small groups to share "books" with their peers. Reading their winning stories is a highlight for the young writers. Awards are not given at the Conference, but are presented in the homerooms or at assemblies in their own school on appropriate occasions.

Primary groups meet in one section during the afternoon, enjoying a music and story time together with primary resource teachers in charge of activities. At the same time, intermediate grades meet with other resource teachers after the small group-sharing sessions, and enjoy some form of entertainment.

This year, an intermediate group of young actors from Mrs. Eloise Ward's fifth grade class from Washington Elementary School, Caldwell, Idaho entertained the Nampa intermediate section.

The young people from Caldwell brought "A Day with Aesop," a puppet presentation of eight well-known Aesop fables. The children themselves wrote the scripts, made the puppets, and designed and constructed the puppet theater which was brought on the bus with them from Caldwell.

Channel 6 television personnel videotaped the activities of the Young Authors Conference whose theme was "a trainload of books for reading," and meeting rooms were colorfully decorated to depict the theme. Programs, name tags, and advance publicity carried out the trainload of books motif.

During the week following the Conference, the children's books were on display in the Nampa Public Library. The children's librarians read the books and selected several that they felt were good for publication. They recommended a publisher of children's books, and some of the award winners will be sent to the publisher.

Educators in the Nampa system believe that every child has a right to develop potential, and that the young authors, artists, musicians, and poets should be encouraged as enthusiastically as the young scientists, naturalists, scholars and athletes. It's a small world, but an exciting one, and such occasions as a young authors' conference have a place in the educational process in Nampa, Idaho.

The Writing Process and the Tape Recorder

Patrick F. Berger

*Teachers of the senior literature courses at
Parkway West Senior High School, Ballwin,
Missouri decided that taped analysis of a
thoroughly known work would stimulate student
writing. Patrick F. Berger, one of the teachers,
tells of their success.*

It was that time of year again — midterm — and the teachers of the senior literature courses were sitting around and voicing the timeless complaints of those who had graded too many papers on the thematic significance of the weeded garden imagery in *Hamlet.*

"How do we get them to see the importance of organization?"

"Why can't they ever develop an idea?"

"If I see one more unsubstantiated generalization...."

Then, of course, there were the usual despairing notes about style, or the lack of it.

We came together in mutual gloom and wondered how we could send them off to college with such a pathetic lack of competence. Finally someone asked, "When do we [teachers] write coherently about literature?" That question stopped everyone.

"Realistically," answered one teacher, "when I have to do a term paper for some summer school course."

"When I want to," said another.

"When I know something extremely well," ventured a third.

So why could we not strive to create within the students just such an atmosphere: the need to write about literature based on the analysis of a text that was thoroughly known. We decided to try the following experiment. We would choose a common piece of literature to be read by all the senior literature classes, whether it be American Literature, English Literature, World Literature, or the Modern Short Story Course. We would choose a piece that would have the most universal appeal and that would, as a result, make the students *want* to write. After the usual squabbling and haggling, we decided on *Death of a Salesman.* Even if an eighteen-year-old could not see himself as an aged, failed salesman, still, we surmised, the students would easily enough realize that Miller was talking about the American Dream of material success, the pitfalls of the business world, the adolescent worship of sports as an end in itself, the loss of innocence suffered by Biff, and the destructive results of a vision not suited to one's talents. So that the students would know the play in detail, we asked them to read a section for homework, then the following day we would play that part in class on tape. After the students heard the play *in toto*, followed it in class from their texts, and read it on their own, we gave them the usual study questions. Then we broke them into small groups of four to six students, gave them a tape recorder, and let them discuss the study questions while being taped. The next day, each group traded its taped session with another group and listened to a different handling of the same questions. Finally, after four days of this, each group obtained its own taped discussion and listened to its original attempt to handle the questions. The next day the entire class, usually consisting of about twenty to twenty-five students per section, reconvened with its teacher, aired further questions and observations, and then heard the teacher wrap up the various interpretations of the play from the discussions and from some of the more renowned secondary sources. Finally, the students were told to pick a topic and write a critical paper.

The reactions of the students to the taped sessions were nothing short of miraculous. They were embarrassed and irate at their bumbling, inarticulate phrasing. Time and again a student would say, "That's not what I meant," or "Do I always sound that vague?" or "To say what's exactly in your mind is really hard, isn't it?" For the first time, the group as a unit felt the need to be precise, to organize ideas, to make coherent connections between thoughts, to fill out generalizations with concrete references to the text, and most of all, to draw a meaningful and logical conclusion from the premises which they had established. Students began to ask themselves why they used such weak examples or such illogical ones to back up what they wanted to prove. They insisted on playing and replaying the tapes. A couple of groups asked whether they could retape their sessions based on what they now knew and felt. They volunteered to come after school and early in the morning to do it. Afterwards, they were so proud that they literally forced their instructors to come in early to hear their new recordings and to grade them. Woe to the teacher who failed to heed their "requests."

Needless to say, the papers were the best products that the senior literature teachers had ever received. Mature, complex, in-depth essays were written about "Linda as Responsible Agent For Willy's Downfall," "The Rejection of the American Financial Dream versus an Equal Rejection of a Marxist Non-competitive Dream," "The Suppressed Pastoral Need of Willy as Source of His Tragic Flaw." Even with these sententious titles, the papers were neither pompous nor trite. They were composed in an organized manner with a beginning, middle, and end. The logic was well beyond what the readers normally found, and curiously, the usual grammatical difficulties like needless change of tense, vague pronoun references, dangling modifiers, and the difficulty of placing main ideas in main clauses and subordinate ideas in subordinate clauses were greatly lessened.

From this experience, we drew some fairly obvious but too-often neglected truisms about the writing process. First, writers must have ideas before they can write. Second, they should be familiar with these ideas and with the text from which they emanate. Third, they cannot express these ideas very clearly unless they have articulated them in prior discussions before others to test the premises, proof, and development of logic. Vague ideas appear in vaguely written essays mainly because they have not been tested and articulated through an oral medium. Fourth, a need has to be created in the writer to express these ideas. Once the students heard themselves mumble vague generalities on the tapes, such a need was created. True, we ran the risk of embarrassing some students, but the teachers were careful to point out beforehand that the purpose of the tape was not to embarrass anyone but to show concretely how difficult precise articulation of an idea can be. We stressed the idea of a mutual need to communicate, not of a superior pontificating to an inferior. The students accepted this premise and were unusually kind to one another.

We also realized that there are no magical formulas that will ensure the success of any writing assignment, but we became increasingly aware that writing is not easy and that perhaps we had done the students a great disservice by not reminding them that writing is a discipline which requires preparation and practice before satisfactory execution.

Methods to Motivate Composition Students

John McIntyre

Ideas that motivated students were based on key concepts in the programs of several well-known English educators. John McIntyre is a lecturer at Syracuse University and assistant coordinator of the West Genesee/Marcellus/Syracuse University Teaching Center.

The development of motivation is a major difficulty of any composition course. In order to develp motivation, a teacher must have a positive attitude toward the students and toward composition in general. Students must be seen as positive, capable beings and the competency and knowledge that they bring to class must be acknowledged. Teachers must also recognize that students can write successfully when they are working on their own ideas. Ideas for writing come from all experiences. In turn, students experience and observe the world around them and absorb these experiences through which thought is stimulated. A successful composition teacher will harness these ideas and will generate a composition program that is innovative, challenging and exciting.

Virginia P. Redd agrees that motivation is the major difficulty in a composition course. Central to this conviction are these principles for creating motivation:

1. The key word in motivation is relevance. As previously stated, a composition class should rely heavily on the experience and ideas of the students. Traditional methods and traditional ideas often fall on "deaf" ears.

2. Students possess a hidden reservoir of interests and experience which must be tapped to provide background for writing. This is a crucial principle for motivating students.

3. A sensitivity to the world around them must be developed within the students. Sensitivity is a prerequisite for effective writing.

4. Techniques for motivating writing must be adjusted to the learning styles of young adolescents.

5. Students are often stimulated by capsulized "mini-writing" exercises.

6. Evaluation by grading is a strong motivating force. This is true in some cases. There are students who are grade-oriented and base their success solely on the grade obtained. However, grading often hinders a student's creativity and should be used sparingly.

One cannot consider writing programs without taking note of the successful program proposed by Dr. Daniel N. Fader. Fader's program, first proposed in *Hooked On Books: Program and Proof,* is based on the dual concepts of *Saturation* and *Diffusion.* Saturation is primarily a reading program. This concept proposes to so surround students with newspapers, magazines, and paperback books that they come to perceive them as pleasurable means to necessary ends. Furthermore, Saturation applies in principle not only to the selection and distribution of periodicals and paperback texts, but to the explosion of writing. In other words, the writing program evolves from the reading program and results in the concept of Diffusion. This refers to the diffusion of English throughout every classroom in the school and results in the English teacher acting as resource person and guide for colleagues. However, one can often expect resistance from colleagues who believe that English should be taught in the English classroom, math in the math classroom and so on. It then becomes the English teacher's responsibility to change the behavior of these colleagues or to revise portions of Fader's program in order to conduct a more specialized writing program.

Dr. Fader has three significant propositions for successful writing programs:

1. the public school student can be taught to write by writing (in quantity and on subjects appropriate to his individual level of attainment);

2. this teaching and writing must not be confined to the English classroom, which has so often been for [the student] a scene of failure and a source of frustration;

3. the nature of the English classroom must be radically altered if it is to play a meaningful part in his education.

The Diffusion program is primarily based on two methods. The first is related to the nongraded program and the practice of requiring students to write papers that no instructor will read. This approach is not so much to get students to write correctly as it is to get students to write. An example of this method would be to require five sets of papers in a two-week period; one set per week is read and commented upon for content by the class instructor, one set every two weeks is corrected for grammar and rhetoric, and one set per week is filed *unread* in the student's folder. This method offers the student an opportunity for performance "by allowing him time to exercise his writing muscles.... — to develop [his] prose-writing muscles to a point where he can use them without fear of aches and strains."

The second method is that of the journal. According to Fader, quantity of production should be the only criterion for judging journal writing. Content, style, grammar, and rhetoric are all insignificant compared to quantity. Consequently, students are told that the only reason for the existence of the journal is to provide them with an opportunity to practice their writing, that the journal will be read only if the teacher is invited to read it, and that the journal will be assessed on quantity only. Also, Fader recommends that the students be allowed to copy. Copying does lead to reading, and most students get bored with copying and advance to another stage of writing. One must remember, however, that Dr. Fader's program must be viewed as a building block in the structure of a student's literacy, and that it is aimed primarily at students who will not write. A similar program would need to be reviewed and revised before submitting the program for use in an advanced composition class.

Another interesting, unique, and effective method is the use of the television commercial as a motivational tool. Familiar TV commercials are admirably suited to illustrate many of the factors that make for effective writing. This statement may at first seem ridiculous, but consider these statements by Richard Lee Smith:

1. TV commercials are brief and usually well written.

2. Commercials are familiar to almost all students, including those whose reading ability and knowledge of literature is markedly deficient.

3. TV commercials belong to the youthful and popular mass culture, rather than the "tiresome" world of school and books.

4. A mature and critical understanding of television and its power and potential would seem to be a necessary part of the intellectual background of an educated citizen.

5. Finally, there is no doubt that a thorough study of television commercials can raise serious esthetic and ethical questions.

One use of TV commercials can be to teach organization in writing and to introduce a general theme outline (Introduction, Body, Conclusion) to a class.

The introduction to a theme or a commercial has two purposes: first, to get the exposition or narrative off on the right track, and second, to arouse interest. The device which the TV copywriter seizes and uses to hold the attention of the viewer is the "grabber." Writing a "grabber" presents the same problem as writing the introductory sentence of a theme; both involve direction and interest. An exercise to introduce the idea of the grabber would be to take a number of body copies from printed ads and to ask the students to write headlines for them. Then compare them to the originals and discuss.

The body of the commercial is called the demonstration. This contains the selling message; it logically presents the arguments that lead the consumer to purchase the product. As a result, the demonstration provides an example of a logical, well-developed argument which supports the premise of the commercial. An excellent example for illustrating the body of a well-written story is evident.

The conclusion of the commercial is the "payoff." The nature of the payoff is determined by the grabber. For example, if the grabber sets up a conflict, the payoff must resolve it. However, the writing of a strong conclusion is not easy. The secret is in advance preparation. The student should have a conclusion well in mind before writing. Thus, the body of the exposition will have some direction. To introduce students to the conclusion/payoff, try having students match premises and conclusions using two-line jokes from an old joke book, or have them return to some of the grabbers and bodies they have previously written and try to make them "pay off" in a consistent yet original manner.

One of the most familiar techniques for motivating composition students is the use of films. In the past, films served as a story-telling device. Contemporary films, however, often appear nonlinear and the viewer must organize disparate ideas and images into meaningful wholes. Since these films allow many interpretations, they offer an intellectual challenge and can be readily employed as stimuli for writing.

In order to help students respond creatively to film stimuli, teachers might follow these suggestions:

1. Provide psychological and physical conditions which facilitate creative effort.

2. Make directions fairly open.

3. Vary instructions with groups and individuals. At times, discussion following the film is good; at other times, immediate writing should follow.

4. Select films judiciously. In order to sustain a particular mood, a film should generally be less than ten minutes. There are obviously some exceptions.

Some films that I have found to be successful are:

American Time Capsule	Red Balloon
Cry of the Marsh	Sixties
Geronimo Jones	Ski Fever
Huntsman	Why Man Creates
Moods of Surfing	Will To Win
Orange and Blue	

I must warn against two things, however. "Mini-film festivals" should not replace composition class. Furthermore, the use of film must be integrated with other approaches; its exclusive use is as damaging as exclusive use of any traditional approach.

One of the points stressed in this article is that composition courses must be relevant to the students. A shortcut to relevancy is to have the students write for a real audience rather than just the teacher. As Stephen Judy points out, "Teachers' obsession with correctness has been one of the major confining structures which have been imposed on the writing class. When students know they are writing for real audiences and know their work will be seen in print, they become more interested in matters of correctness." There are numerous ways to find a real audience for student writing. Three of the more successful are:

1. School newspapers are usually clamoring for material. Have your students write articles, stories, etc. that will be submitted to the newspaper. Nothing can change a student's sour attitude toward writing more than having his or her writing accepted and praised by peers.

2. If your school does not have a newspaper, make as many copies of your students' work as possible and distribute throughout the school.

3. A very successful method in motivating students is money, and the *Writer's Market* is one source of this motivation. This is a collection of all the magazines that will accept material from the public. These magazines run the gamut from *Esquire* to *Jack 'n Jill*. Although the monetary rewards are slim, the motivational impact on the students is immeasureable.

Obviously, if a student is to be motivated, the composition assignment should be a good one. Gilbert Tierney and Stephen Judy have developed a list of questions for assessing the criteria for a good writing assignment. I have condensed their list below:

Criteria Concerning the Writer and the Structure of the Assignment

- Motivation and Stimulation. Does the assignment provide enough direction? Does it avoid channelling all students into the same kind of composition? Is the activity one for which the students have enough knowledge to write freely? Is the assignment interesting and rewarding?
- Appropriateness. Are the subject and form appropriate for the age, maturity, and background of your students?
- Open-endedness. Is a divergence of forms and responses allowed? Are there options for students of varying abilities and interests?
- Language Play. Is the assignment designed to encourage the students to try something new?

Criteria Concerning the Writer and His Audience

- The Writer's Function. Is the student helped to see kinds of roles and possible approaches that are open to him as a writer?

- Voice. Is the student asked to write in a voice that is natural to him? Is he allowed to make clear his attitude toward his audience and his subject?
- Readers. Is a real audience, one important to the writer, provided for the paper?
- Reactions. Are provisions made for the members of the audience to talk to the writer about the paper? Can he develop a sense of pleasure and satisfaction over showing his work to others?

Perhaps the most important contributing factor to motivation is the necessity of a classroom atmosphere where students know they can say what they honestly think but where ideas will be examined impartially and critically. The teacher should start with content at the level of the student's interests and abilities. In the beginning, students best communicate matters of particular concern to them. Through the impact of literature and discussion, these concerns extend and deepen. The teacher who is growing, both in mastery of subject and in understanding of adolescents, can devise many ways to release this vitality of thought.

References

Dauterman, Philip and Robert Stahl. "Film Stimuli—An Approach to Creative Writing." *English Journal*, 60 (November 1971), 1120–1122.

Fader, Daniel N. and Elton B. McNeil. *Hooked on Books: Program and Proof.* New York: Berkley, 1968.

Judy, Stephen N. "The Search for Structures in the Teaching of Composition." *English Journal*, 59 (February 1970), 213–218.

Loban, Walter, Margaret Ryan, and James Squire. "Written Expression." *Teaching Language and Literature*, New York, Harcourt, Brace & World, 1969, 319–377.

Redd, Virginia P. "Teaching Writing in the Junior High School." *English Journal*, 59 (April 1970), 540–47.

Smith, Richard Lee. "Tired of Reading Disorganized Themes? For Quick Relief Try TV Commercials." *The Clearing House*, 47 (December 1972), 223–28.

Tierney, Gilbert and Stephen N. Judy. "The Assignment Makers." *English Journal*, 61 (February 1972), 265–69.

Finding a Subject

Tales, Tots, and Treasures

Bonnie Smith Schulwitz

Certain classroom experiences inspired imaginative poems and stories in the creative writing workshops conducted by Central Michigan University for Saginaw-area children. Bonnie Smith Schulwitz is associate professor there.

Creative expression in all phases of the language arts is enhanced by a child's direct experience. Illustrating the value of direct experience for the language arts, the question might be asked, "What is a blind person?" The reply could be, "A blind person is a person who cannot see." Alternatively, the reply could be, "Close your eyes and, keeping them closed all the time, try to find your way out of this room." The first answer contains concise and accurate information; the mind is possibly satisfied. But the second answer leads the inquirer to moments of direct experience, transcending mere knowledge, enriching the imagination, possibly touching the heart and soul as well as the mind.[1]

In providing direct experience for a child, the teacher of creative writing establishes a concrete base from which that child can express creative thought. The direct experience helps to form the vital impression from which the creative expression can flow. While direct experience can function in many forms to ensure success in the creative writing it evokes, I'd like to share three successful ways we have utilized it, illustrating corresponding examples of the children's creative writing products.

Direct Experience with Poetry Forms

Structured forms of poetry successfully initiate poetry writing with children of all ages. Our poetry sessions often begin with one-line poetry, unhampered by any requirement of meter or rhyme. "Happiness is . . . ," "Sadness is . . . ," or "Relief is . . ." provide a good beginning:

> "Relief is finding your report before your teacher kills you."

> "Relief is knowing you can outrun your enemies."

> "Relief is getting out of school before your teacher remembers you were supposed to stay after."

---

[1] Brian Way, *Development through Drama* (London: Longman Group Limited, 1967).

28

"Relief is a good teacher."

A structured poetry form, like the cinquain, may provide just the support a child needs to create a poem. It is a 5 line, 22 syllable (2,4,6,8,2) structure, following a distinct line pattern:

line 1: the title
line 2: describes the title
line 3: expresses an action
line 4: expresses a feeling
line 5: indicates another word for the title.

Using this format, one six year old wrote:

Puppy
Warm and fuzzy
Sniffing, running, flopping
When I touch her head I feel warm
Sadie

Direct Experience with Common Events

Many teachers incorporate a feast of some type in conjunction with a particular unit of study or a time of the year. One group of nine-year-olds planned a Halloween feast culminating the intensive study of this holiday with its proverbial collection of ghosts, ghouls, and goblins. One creatively concocted menu for a Halloween feast read:

What Ghosts Eat

Green ghostlosh and ghost toasties
Horrorbel Halloween hamburgers
Old owl omelettes
Sick soup
Terrible toast
Spookgetti

Any school or classroom event builds concrete and common direct experience for story writing. One school-wide project at Coulter School, Saginaw, Michigan involved planting and cultivating a tomato garden in the schoolyard. This activity not only provided experiences in planting, nurturing, and harvesting the tomatoes, but in making tomato soup, juice, and chili. Throughout the entire project the teachers found many ways to integrate the experiences with curricular areas of study. Many language arts activities evolved, including creative short stories. For example, one boy wrote:

Tomato Juice
I like tomato juice. I had fun making it.
It was differnt fun. But I had three glasses of
it. And I hated it. Only *one* glass of it is ok.

Direct Experience with Literary Forms

Books, stories, or poems with repetitious language patterns are enjoyable "story starters" for children. Remy Charlip's *What Good Luck! What Bad Luck!*[2] inspired Jerry's story which began,

> What good luck, it's Saturday,
> What bad luck, it's raining,
> What good luck, we'll play with the toss game,
> What bad luck, the dog ate it...

Did You Ever See? by Walter Einsel[3] is another example for stimulating unique interpretations.

Personalized interpretations of fables, fairy tales, and nursery rhymes appeal even to older students. Teenagers created the following:

Little Ms. Muffet

Little Ms. Muffet
Sat on a tuffet
Eating her curds and whey
Because she was groovie
She took a guy to a horror movie
Which frightened the poor guy away.

Big Man Blue

Big Man Blue come play your guitar
The people out there will make you a star
Where's the guy who makes the neat sound?
He's in the sack with dreams all around.

Marverella

Not very long ago, Freddy, the son of the U.S. President, decided to have a rock concert, which was to be held at Washington Square Garden. Everyone, and I do mean everyone was invited!

Now somewhere in Washington, D.C. there lived a fair maiden named Marverella. Marverella was a lovely girl, but lo and behold, she had two wicked step-sisters, Fenicia and Lucretia, and a wicked step-mother.

Marverella should have been allowed to go out on dates and have a jolly good time but her wicked step-mother and sisters made her do all the work. She had to scrub the floors, wash and iron clothes, do the dishes, dusting, wash windows, and make the beds. With all this work, she had no time for herself.

---

[2] Remy Charlip, *What Good Luck! What Bad Luck!* (New York: Scholastic Book Services, 1970).

[3] Walter Einsel, *Did You Ever See?* (New York: Scholastic Book Services, 1962).

It happened that one day Fenicia and Lucretia came home bubbling with enthusiasm. "Why are you so excited?" exclaimed Marverella. "Freddy, the son of the President is having a rock concert, and everyone is invited. Isn't that the grooviest thing that you ever heard?"

"Far out," exclaimed Marverella. "Can I go too?"

"Ha, Ha! Out a sight! Marverella of all people wants to go to the rock concert! Well the answer is no. You must do the work and help us get ready for the joyful event," the wicked sisters replied.

At last the day of the rock concert came. Lucretia and Fenicia had beautiful garments but still were as ugly as sin.

After their departure, Marverella sat down and cried her heart out. Suddenly, out of no where someone appeared. "Why are you crying my pretty child?"

"I want to go to Freddy's rock concert, but . . . but who are you?"

"I am Samantha, and I am here to bewitch you. You will go to Freddy's rock concert and you will have a ball!"

Samantha twitched her nose and Cinda's hair was styled into the newest look—the gypsy. Samantha waved her witchly finger and Marverella's garments were changed into lovely bell bottom blue jeans and a smock top. Samantha twitched her nose again and Cinda had on a lovely pair of mod boots.

"Oh I can't believe it," shouted Marverella. "I'm going to the rock concert after all."

But lo and behold, how was she to get there? Suddenly, a Honda motorcycle appeared in the front yard and Marverella roared off gallantly after she thanked Samantha.

When Marverella arrived at the rock concert Freddy saw her immediately and fell in love with her. Marverella impressed him even more than the Credence Clearwater Revival, the Rolling Stones, and The Who. About one o'clock in the morning Freddy got up the nerve to ask Marverella to marry him. She said "yes" at once.

At this very time, somewhere in Washington, D.C. they are living in a GM Mobile Home. They decided on this because living in a GM Mobile Home means never having to say you're sorry!

These examples of direct experience and creative writing will hopefully build your own precious mixture of "tales, tots, and treasures."

A Slide Show Travelogue

Richard L. Hanzelka

Children wanted to write when the activities centered around convincing their parents of a good place to spend a vacation. The project was headed by Richard L. Hanzelka, K-12 language arts coordinator, Mississippi Bend Area Education Agency, Davenport, Iowa.

While working during a recent summer with a group of low-achieving students in language arts and reading, I had success with an activity which developed at least three kinds of composition skills: letter writing, summarizing material, and script writing. Materials needed for the activity include:

1. Kodak Ektagraphic Visualmaker (this kit is equipped with a mounted Instamatic Kodak camera) *or* a 35mm camera mounted on a stand *or* a competent A-V resource person.

2. One or two newspapers which include a quantity of travel advertisements for exciting, colorful vacations. The *New York Times* and *Chicago Tribune* are especially good for this. Several travel magazines are also useful.

3. Carousel slide projector

4. Tape recorder

The series of procedures described below can be expanded or compressed depending on the teaching situation. Since the basic purposes are better writing, summarizing, and scripting, it is usually necessary to spend time in a writing workshop situation so that students can get suggestions from each other as well as from the teacher.

1. Cut out all advertisements and coupons which offer free brochures about scenic vacation areas.

2. Have each student select one or two interesting resort or vacation spots and write letters requesting any *colorful* brochures for the class activity. Some students may want to send the clip-out coupon without a letter. At that point the teacher can either explain that the letter is part of the assignment or that a better response may be obtained if the people know the information is to be used in a school project.

3. After the letters have been sent, move on to another activity for two weeks or so while responses to letters come in. It is a good idea for the

teacher to write to five or ten leftover vacation spots as well, in case some returns are very slow or never show up.

4. When information has been received from the vacation spots, each student should select five to ten good pictures from the brochures. Using one of the methods described in the materials section above, 2″ x 2″ slides should be made of those pictures.

5. Students should summarize, rewrite, and quote materials from the brochures in an effort to explain their vacation sites in travelogue fashion in conjunction with the slides they have selected. The teacher should not make assumptions about students' understanding of travelogues nor should it be assumed that students will know how to summarize immediately.

6. The summarized material should be written in script form and practiced on tape until the student feels comfortable with it.

7. An overall theme and title for the travelogue can be determined by the class. In addition, background music selected by the teacher or by a student committee is also effective. In order to ensure that effective transitions are made between segments, additional oral or visual bridges may be created.

8. After several practice sessions, make a final tape, organize the slides, and buy some popcorn. Then invite the parents, serve them popcorn and let them plan their next several vacations from the visual experiences provided by your students.

9. If student interest is still high, several extensions and enrichment activities are possible, e.g. making posters and collages, writing stories with a particular vacation spot as the setting, or writing poems and songs about the vacation spots.

The best part of this writing activity is that it is not a "dummy run," but truly "language in operation."

Getting Started with Want Ads

Robert A. McKeag

Selecting a topic seems a universally difficult problem for student writers. Robert A. McKeag has used a "want ad" solution at the University of Wisconsin, Oshkosh.

Selecting a topic is often the most difficult part of a writing assignment. A team of student teachers and I tried one solution with a high school level creative writing class. We used classified want ads to get students to select and define topics and begin writing. A want ad approach has the advantage of credibility. Kids know such ads are used in the "real world" to get things done, and this approach also gives the students some choices without being suffocatingly narrow or so broad that direction is lost. It is useful to begin with a discussion of want ads and how they are used to locate people and things and to accomplish a specific purpose. Then follow the discussion by distributing a mimeographed sheet of paper which reads as follows:

For the next few weeks, we will give you a chance to work on a writing unit of your choice. Read the course descriptions below and choose the unit which interests you most!

1. WANTED: Prospective Shakespeares. *Playwrights.* Using examples from the drama unit in the textbook, write an original play or adapt a short story or situation to dramatic form with the possibility that it may be acted out. This could be a group effort.

2. WANTED: Cecil B. Demilles-to-be (or not to be). *Movie Writers.* Prepare a written film script on a short subject, make your own film complete with sound or voice background. This will cost you something (the price of the film and processing). No pornography, please. This could be a group effort.

3. WANTED: Dr. Suesses or Mother Gooses. *Children's Book Writers.* Read twenty children's stories, preferably Caldecott or Newberry award winners, and write one of your own designed for a certain age group. Do or suggest illustrations for each page. When your masterpiece is completed, present it to a class of elementary children. (We will make arrangements and provide transportation.)

4. WANTED: Mad Scientists willing to record their fantasies in the manner of Ray Bradbury, Issac Asimov, or Robert Heinlein. *Science Fiction Writers*. Read selected science fiction and write a story of your own which makes the improbable seem probable.

5. WANTED: Afternoon TV watchers. *Soap Opera Writers*. Relying on your knowledge of current television soap operas, write an essay describing the soap opera as a current type of literature and explain why it is so popular. Then write a half-hour production (complete with commercials) which meets the criteria you describe in your essay and produce it on video tape or audio tape. This could be a group effort.

6. WANTED: Someone to commit the perfect crime on paper (and solve it). *Detective Story Writers*. Inspired by Ellery Queen, Mickey Spillaine, Sir Arthur Conan Doyle and Agatha Christie, write a who-dun-it to end all who-dun-its.

7. WANTED: Superman and Wonder Woman. *Comic Book Writers*. Spend a few days reading the leftover comic books in your attic. Then create your own character and launch him on a fantastic adventure. You don't have to be a Rembrandt, but you will have to draw well enough so that this looks like a real comic book. Color is optional.

8. WANTED: Hidden Persuaders to experiment with propaganda. *Ad Agency Persons*. Crooked Use of Straight English. Select an idea, such as school is good for you, and convince the class using propaganda techniques to include loaded language, semantic skullduggery, unsupported inferences and other slanted techniques. Prepare and present a half-hour program using posters, news articles, ads and other media to get your point across.

Please choose three units you would like to try, ranked according to preference:

1.
2.
3.
NAME_____

We found that the want ad approach to student writing worked very well in assisting students with the difficult task of getting started and selecting a topic. Students view the "ads" much like course descriptions in a college catalog and choose on the basis of the requirements of the task involved as well as their own preferences. The description of the job requirements provides a general idea of what will likely be required in the writing but leaves the expanding and detailing up to the students. Filling in details and expanding generalities are a major portion of what writing is all about. Once the controlling idea, or "grand design," is established, students are free to move on to the actual task of writing. It can be claimed that writing skills are developed by the actual task of writing, so it would seem that any help we can give students in jumping that first big hurdle will pay off in better writing and more practice at writing.

Folklife: An Unlimited Writing Source

Raymond J. Rodrigues

Tapping the folklife surrounding the student, as the "Foxfire" projects proved, can make a writing program come alive. Raymond J. Rodrigues, assistant professor at the University of Utah, Salt Lake City, tells how to go about it.

The success of Eliot Wigginton's "Foxfire" books has inspired many teachers to send their students to the older members of the community to collect folktales, historical tidbits, and how-to-do-it lessons. Some teachers have backed off from such projects, fearing that their community simply does not have the resources which Appalachia has. Nevertheless, if we treat "folklore" as "folklife," the current practices and traditions of the people, then we open up as writing sources virtually everything which surrounds the student.

Folk research need not be confined to books, for life in every community is filled with traditions to which students are exposed and which they may study with effort ranging from minimal to maximum. No longer must the teacher wonder whether students can find sources for their projects, whether their after-school obligations, however serious or wasteful, will prevent them from gathering the data for compositions, oral or written. Folklife, as a study in itself, consists of examining anything which has in any way been systematized through tradition, involving all the variations upon that systematization.

Students can begin with the most familiar sources available to them, their families and friends. From examining the traditions practiced by these groups, they can branch out into the surrounding community and find tradition all around them. They may even find those older individuals who can talk about the past, who still practice traditional arts and crafts, and who will spin fascinating yarns.

The list below is but a sampler of the types of traditions students can investigate. Some are extremely ordinary and may not initially appeal to those students who demand the exotic. Still others require much research. But by developing ideas which will relate to specific communities and classes, the teacher will find much for the students to write about.

   1. *Childcare:* How are children reared? Which parent has the primary responsibility for caring for the child? Where do children sleep,

37

eat, and play? What types of games and toys are children allowed? How are babysitters selected and instructed?

2. *Education:* How are schools built? What are some typical attitudes of students toward school and teachers? Did the parents of the students feel the same way when they were in school? How does the community control its schools? Are curricula in all schools alike? Which courses must all students have?

3. *Extracurricular activities:* Examine the uniforms of the teams, bands, and other student groups. How different or similar are they from school to school? Why? Are there traditional activities for girls? For boys?

4. *Food and eating:* What is a typical meal? Where are utensils actually placed on the table? What times do people eat? Where? Who is served first? Do families continue the foods and cooking techniques of their ancestors?

5. *Dating:* Where do people go? What is a good date? Did the students' parents have similar dates? Who initiates the date?

6. *Immigrants:* Where did they come from? What traditions did they bring with them? Has the first generation born here kept any of those traditions?

7. *Architecture:* Describe traditional architectural styles and materials in your community. Do many houses have a similar design? Are they exactly alike or are there variations? What types of windows are in the homes? How do they work? Are the roofs flat or peaked? How much? Why? Where is the kitchen? Is there a porch?

8. *Publications:* Is the local newspaper always put together in the same way? Go back and look at old issues. What elements are the same as in the current issues? What has changed? Why?

9. *Gardens, indoor and out:* What do people grow? How? Where are gardens placed? How are indoor plants displayed?

10. *Community government:* How do the elected and nonelected officials arrive at their positions? Has your community always had the same type of government? Do people learn how their local government functions, or do they ignore it?

11. *Names:* Do many families have the same last name? Where did they come from? Are those names found around the community: streets, schools, rivers, parks? How are people named? How are pets named? Schools?

12. *Holidays:* Examine a particular holiday. How do people celebrate it? Do they employ decorations? Where? What kinds? Are there formal public ceremonies? Who is in charge? Is there a traditional celebration which only your community celebrates?

13. *Languages:* How many are spoken in your community? By whom? When? Where? Why? How did they get there?

Since students write more meaningfully when they have a special audience to write for, suggesting that they find some medium for "publishing" their findings should inspire them to improve their communications, one of the teacher's primary goals.

Writing Skills for Junior High

Debra A. Tinker
Vandalia, Ohio

Writing skills are *not* limited to composition only, although that is what frequently comes to mind. Writing should be considered a means of personal or mass communication in the form of a letter, cartoon, poem, short story, play, etc. Junior high students are exposed to many forms of writing within even a limited curriculum; the activities in a junior high writing program must be diversified. Within each "child-student" there is a wealth of imaginative creativity.

Usually, I commence the school year with the study of the short story, since I find it easy to relate this to other forms of writing. For example, radio plays made from Poe stories are easily obtainable on cassette tapes, as are those of other famous authors. After studying a few short stories, I have the students listen to and discuss one of the plays, and the various techniques employed in telling the same story two different ways. Then the students form groups, and with a bit of guidance, write their own radio plays from one of the other stories. They write scripts, changing narration in the story to sound effects and dialogue, and are only permitted to use an announcer for the Master of Ceremonies. When completed, the plays are rehearsed and performed!

On performance day, I put up a giant radio, drawn on a large piece of newsprint. The performers sit behind this with a cassette player and a phonograph, provided for recorded sound effects. The outcome can be pretty fantastic, with commercials and all!

Then there is the newspaper. Activities utilizing the newspaper as a resource are practically unlimitable. There are many different writing skills demonstrated in any edition. There are articles to inspire the would-be journalist, and editorials with which to study essay techniques. Letters to the editor can be useful in teaching not only letter writing, but also argumentation. There is advertising of all kinds, written sports interviews, and naturally, the all-time favorite — the comics. (Students really enjoy writing their own comics, and it is an amusing way to learn conciseness.)

A good first-day-of-school activity is the newspaper-inspired interview game. This is particularly enjoyable in a seventh-grade class where there are so many strangers. Have the students pair up (preferably stranger-to-stranger to encourage new friendships) and interview each other. It is best to suggest leading questions for them, or all you may end up with is "name, rank, and serial number." After they have had approximately five minutes to chat, have each interviewer introduce their "guest" to the rest of the class. When everyone has been introduced, each student may either write up the interview or write a short biography. I have found this to be a great icebreaker.

Composition is another method of opening communication lines in the classroom. The very first composition my class writes is a group project. I write three incomplete leading sentences on the board, and each student chooses one with which to begin his or her own paper. An example would be, "I dashed around the corner and who should I run smack into, but . . . ." The class has three minutes to write all they can before I call "time," when they pass their paper to someone else. The next writer has four minutes to read the paper and continue the story. Papers change hands once more before collection. I usually read them all, then read the most interesting ones the next day.

A similar activity, but more individualized, is the open-ended story. This is where the teacher provides the class with half of a story and lets them finish it. You may either make up the beginning or use a previously published one. Another idea is to use the beginning of a complete story and compare the author's ending with the students'. Then discuss the different effects the different endings may have on the reader.

If junior high students become successful in their writing abilities and verbal communication skills, they will discover much of the self-confidence needed to survive in the contemporary world.

Developing Point of View: Sensing an Audience

Writing about Literature: Eighth Graders Encounter "The Ransom of Red Chief"

Lee Odell and Joanne Cohick

Viewing their texts with a "camera eye," students enjoyed writing with an awareness of the selective nature of perception. Lee Odell teaches at the State University of New York at Buffalo and Joanne Cohick teaches at Oak Harbor Junior High School, Oak Harbor, Washington.

English teachers at almost all grade levels frequently try to combine composition and the study of literature. Sometimes they assign creative writing that uses a literary text as a starting point: Given the sequences of events in this story, write an adequate ending; given what you know about a character in a story or the speaker in a poem, imagine how he or she would think and act in a new situation. At other times, teachers ask for analytic or expository writing in which students summarize plots, describe characters, or discuss theme. Each kind of assignment has its uses, but each is a little unsatisfactory. The former tends to lead away from the text; too often it does not help students think carefully about what's actually on the page in front of them. The latter asks students to examine the text, but it often produces essays that seem sterile, mechanical, devoid of the feelings and associations that accompany a full response to a work of literature.

As one means of overcoming these difficulties, we suggest that students do a different sort of writing about literature, writing that asks them to examine a text closely and to use their imagination to give meaning to the words on the page. The following activity, used recently with a group of eighth graders, illustrates this point.

As an introduction to the project, students were given the following homework assignment: watch a dramatic program (as opposed to a variety show or "special") on television and count the number of times the television camera changes focus (i.e., the distance and angle from which pictures were taken) during a two-minute period. During class the next day, students commented on how much the camera seemed to move — zooming in to catch the look on someone's face, pulling back to show other characters' reactions, drawing back still farther to show the physical surroundings in which action was taking place. Students next examined comic strips in which the writer/artist made frequent changes in focus. They paid considerable attention to the way these changes emphasized visual details; they noted, for example, how a close-up shot called attention to the lines in a character's face that might suggest age and worry. For at least half a class period, students either listed visual details that were included in a given frame of a comic strip, or speculated about the visual qualities of objects or people that were only partly shown in the frame.

After examining changes in focus in the television programs and in comic strips, students read the O. Henry short story, "The Ransom of Red Chief." On finishing the story, they were asked to choose one scene they especially liked and to try to visualize that scene, thinking of it as a succession of frames or camera shots in a television program. The ability to draw well, students were assured, was not the main concern. They were to sketch their frames as best they could, but the important thing was the half page of explanation that was to accompany each frame. In these written comments, students were to describe everything that one might see if the image were to appear on a television screen.

Students seemed to appreciate the basic premise of the story: two likeable but inept villians (Sam and Bill) kidnap a young boy (Johnny Dorset) who proves to be a much greater threat to their well-being than they are to his. The following excerpts from papers by Joy, Greg, Karen, and Marsha will illustrate the writing this story elicited. Unfortunately, we can reproduce only a limited amount of the drawing students did.

Joy chose to deal with the scene in which Johnny (who has decided to take on the role and name of "Red Chief") decides to scalp Bill as he lies sleeping. The first frame shows Sam, in the foreground, being awakened by the scuffling of Red Chief and Bill, who are in the background of the picture. Her description of Frame 1:

> Sam's face is sort of stunned and tired at the same time. Bill is moaning and screaming and trying to struggle away from Red Chief. All you can see of Red Chief is the back of his body and his hand up in the air with the knife. The cave is dark and gloomy. The floor is pure dust, maybe a few pebbles here and there. The walls of the cave are of black rocks which are very jagged and have spiders and cobwebs mixed.

Frame 2:

> The camera is now focused on a closer shot of Bill and Red Chief. The camera is facing them at a low, straight-on angle.
> Red Chief has a big devilish grin on his face, just like a devil has when he greets a new member to the group. His hand is tightly clutching the knife, waiting for the right moment to strike.
> Bill's lying there tense as a father to be, in the waiting room. Every once in a while he gets up enough courage to yell out a sound of some kind. His shirt is soaking wet.

Frame 3:

The camera is at an angle view from where [Bill] was, so you can see what Bill was going through, having to look at Red Chief.

[Bill] is super nervous about the knife in [Red Chief's] hand, and [Red Chief's] face isn't helping anything either. Those glassy bloodshot eyes glaring right into his. And [Red Chief's] face is as red as a person holding his breath just before it turns blue. His devilish grin made [Bill's] stomach turn. And [Red Chief's] teeth were crooked and jagged and spaced far apart. It made [Bill] think of a vampire with a lot of teeth missing. [Red Chief's] hot breath, breathing right into [Bill's] face, made him sweat heavily.

In the final frame, Joy has the camera move back, allowing Sam to come into the picture once again.

> Sam's back is partly turned toward the camera, showing only half his face. His longjohn shirt is bulging with the strain of trying to pull Red Chief away from Bill. His white teeth are gritted together as though trying to lift a 500 pound weight. You can't see much of Red Chief.

As she would no doubt be the first to admit, Joy has little future as a commercial artist. But like many of her classmates, Joy is accomplishing one of the basic objectives of the assignment; in successive frames, she makes appropriate shifts in the angle and distance from which she looks at things. In working with the same scene, several of Joy's classmates created somewhat different sequences of frames. While remaining consistent with the text, their work reflected their individual perceptions of what was important in the scene. Their papers suggest that they're beginning to understand a basic point about perception: it is selective, not passive. When we look at an object, a scene, a person, we don't simply stand still and let things come into our line of vision. We move our attention about, selecting and shaping what we perceive. We actively guide our own seeing.

This active perception is apparent not only in frames students drew but also in the syntax of their sentences. In Joy's description of the cave, Frame 1, there are some interesting changes in the grammatical focus (i.e., the grammatical subject) of several of her sentences. The subject of the first sentence is *the cave*. Subsequent sentences focus on (have as their grammatical subject) different aspects of the cave — *the floor* and *the walls*. In describing Frame 3, Joy focuses not just on Red Chief, but on Red Chief's face, his "glassy, bloodshot eyes," his teeth. In both passages, the grammatical subjects of many of the clauses suggest a succession of images, much as though a camera were, literally, focusing first on one significant detail, then on another, then on another.

These changes in grammatical focus (changes that appear not just in Joy's work, but in the writing of most of Joy's classmates on this assignment) suggest that she is taking a lively, sensitive look at things. They are also significant because a change in grammatical focus implies a change in commitment for the rest of the sentence. If Joy had simply remarked, "Red Chief's grin was devilish," she would have had a complete sentence with no syntactic reason to comment further on Red Chief's grin. But by making *Red Chief's devilish grin* the subject of her sentence, she obligates herself to make some additional observation. Just to complete the sentence, she has to think further about her subject. In this particular case, Joy's choice of grammatical focus leads her beyond a statement about a character's physical appearance to a conclusion about how that appearance affects another character.

Not only did Joy and her classmates take a very active, imaginative look at scenes they'd selected, they also created a number of striking analogies — perhaps as one means of compensating for their lack of artistic ability. In the passages we mentioned earlier, Joy remarked that Red Chief was grinning "just like a devil when he greets a new member to the group." In his account of the same scene, Greg observed that "when Bill first arrived at the cave, his hair was like silk. Now with what is going on [Red Chief has Bill pinned to the ground] it feels like wet sandpaper from the slimy water dripping from the ceiling and from the dirt Red Chief has rubbed in his hair." In describing one of her frames Marsha imagined Red Chief sneaking up on Bill with an "expression on his face such as a bird might have when he catches his first worm."

Students' ability to shift focus and to create analogies seems important for two reasons. First, it suggests that students are visualizing the text in some detail and are seeing relationships between that detail and their own experience. In doing so, we feel, students are improving their understanding of the story. Second, students are developing basic composition skills that are important in both "creative" and argumentative/expository writing. They are learning to make comparisons that will help a reader understand the point they wish to make. Moreover, they are gaining the ability to select detail that will create a unified impression or justify a conclusion. This latter ability is shown in all the papers, but it becomes especially clear in Karen's description of one of her frames.

> In this frame I only want to focus on Bill's face. We can see a small cut and bruise on his left temple (of course, Red Chief did it). His cheeks are flushed, his eyes are watering and bloodshot. His lips are cracked and his mouth is open in surprise. He is both surprised and in pain.

Standing by itself, Karen's conclusion ("He is both surprised and in pain") would seem rather unremarkable. However, it occurs at the end of a series of clauses that focus on Bill's cheeks, eyes, etc. In this context, her conclusion seems reasonable, well-founded, sensitive.

Students' written evaluations suggest both the difficulties and the unique value of the sort of work we've been describing. Almost all students mentioned having some problem in doing the work. Several felt, at least briefly, some misgivings about the quality of their art work, and others wrote they were not, at first, exactly sure how to do the writing that accompanied each frame. During the four class periods students spent drawing and describing frames, many students' problems were solved as the teacher went around the room, talking with individuals, reassuring them about their drawing ability, reminding them of the sort of detail the class had pointed out in discussions of comic strips, and showing examples of others' work. For some students, however, the assignment presented difficulties that are not so easily overcome. In her written evaluation, one student observed: "First of all, I liked the story but think that the person who wrote it could have put in more detail. That is where I had all the trouble — putting in all the detail." Another commented: "To me there isn't much to tell about some kid going down a road with a field on both sides. I guess you have to have a big imagination!"

Indeed, to read or write well, one must have a "big imagination." One must be able to go beyond the information given and see relationships, make associations, and complete scenes that may be only partially explicit. This assignment helps identify students (not always the "poorer" students, by the way) who are having difficulty in doing this. And it provides a way to help them develop their reading and writing ability. To do the drawings, students had to look closely at the text and also make use of their own experiences. The drawings, in turn, provided a basis for the writing. By looking at details in the pictures they had drawn, students began to find out what they wanted to say. For some students, the drawing helped generate really interesting metaphors. For others, drawing helped solve the more rudimentary — but equally important — problem of simply discovering what aspects of the story they would write about.

Despite experiencing difficulties (most of them only momentary), almost all students reported that they really enjoyed the work. The most grudging appreciation of the project was that it was "sorta fun." Students seemed to see the point of the activity and wanted to have this sort of assignment again. And one student, Karen, went well beyond the immediate composition exercise to make a sophisticated point about the creative process:

> At first I couldn't think of a thing. So I would just sit there and think hard. The harder I thought, the more my mind would wander. Finally, while I was doing something completely different, something would pop into my head. It's like an oil well. You're drilling hard. Then when you're least expecting it, it'll all gush out.

Karen's comment provides a nice metaphor for the work we've been describing. We can't guarantee that any series of tasks will inevitably lead students to read and write more perceptively. But the procedures we've presented do suggest one way we might help students to begin drilling and allowing the oil to flow.

Help! I'm a Prisoner in a Letter Factory!

Carole Berlin and Nancy Miller

Two seventh grade teachers at different schools got their students excited about writing to each other. Carole Berlin and Nancy Miller teach in New Orleans, Louisiana at Eleanor McMain Secondary Magnet School and L. J. Peters Middle School, respectively.

If you would enjoy having students do *un*assigned homework just for fun; if you'd like your students to *want* to read what's actually on the page (as opposed to what they think ought to be there); if you'd like to see a real improvement in all writing-related skills "happen" to your students — then our writing project is for you.

It is essentially a pen pal project done in stages. It can be duplicated anywhere two teachers in different schools in the same city are willing to try a totally different approach to writing, willing to refrain from grading papers, and willing to let their students teach each other.

We told our students they were going to write letters to students in another part of the city, and laid out the following rules:

1. Students must write profiles giving their name, age, sex, teacher, English period and school, plus two things they love and two things they hate. In addition, they may put in anything they feel would be of interest to a student in another school.
2. Each profile must be answered by a letter from at least one student from the other school.
3. Each first letter received must be answered; after that, the decision to continue the correspondence with that person becomes optional. However, if a student chooses not to continue corresponding, he or she is obligated to inform the other person in a brief letter.
4. Grades will be assigned purely on the basis of quantity: the more letters you write and receive, the higher your grade will be. (The rationale was that if ten people responded to your one profile, you had done a better job of communicating your personality to others than had someone whose profile received only one or two answers; your grade, therefore, should be correspondingly higher.)

They began to write with the understanding that the profile had to follow the form on the board, and be long enough to tell what the students felt was interesting and unique about themselves. The fact that these profiles were to be read by strangers had a profound effect on our students. They had shared their writings with others in class before, but they had been among friends. This was *real*. This was *serious*. Writing about themselves to receive a response from "out there" made them throw themselves into the task with unaccustomed seriousness of purpose.

At the end of the profile-writing session, the students expressed curiosity about the profiles their classmates had written. We decided to play a guessing game the next day, to see if we could tell who had written which profile. It turned out to be one of the highlights of the project for both students and teachers. Some students' names were very easy to guess correctly; Kristina C. wrote, "I am boy-crazy" and immediately, above the laughter, came, "That's got to be Kristina!" Others who had very little to say were chided by their classmates.

With much pleased blushing and shy/bold-eyed listening to their classmates' comments, those who had written too little to be honestly revealing of themselves added to their profiles. These were reread aloud in small clusters, with much giggling. When they asked permission to add, on the backs of their friends' profiles, things like "She's a very loyal friend," or "He always share his food with you," it was granted with amazed delight. How often do students *ask permission* to write more than the minimum? Witnessing this, those who'd never considered revising written works suddenly wanted *their* papers returned to change or to add to. The atmosphere in the classroom took on the flavor and sound of coffee perking happily away.

Two days after the profiles were begun, they were mailed. The very next morning, students ran in asking, "Did we get any mail yet?" A brief description of the time factor in the postal system was tendered, and work began.

When the profiles finally did arrive, we shared them in a variety of ways. One was to string a clothesline across one wall, attaching profiles with spring-type clothespins. As students completed their other assignments, they were able to read profiles without disturbing others. Some students, however, took profiles and didn't return them — a distinct disadvantage for a student whose profile was taken.

We also tried spreading the profiles out on the library tables. Students moved eagerly from table to table, reading profiles, sharing, searching out those that had the most appeal for them. More advanced students got into groups of five or six, each with a batch of profiles. After fifteen minutes, groups swapped profiles, giving everyone a chance to read them all. This method didn't proceed as smoothly as anticipated, however, for bursts of laughter from one group had kids from the others running over to see what was so funny. Derisive comments flew: "These chirrun can't hardly spell they own school right!" Kids ran up to ask what this or that word was. The excitement ran high.

Below-average classes requested that the teacher read the profiles aloud.

Rosaline Conery
Miss Miller
Period II

Dear Mr Main
Hello Mc Main I am
in the seventh grade. I am
13 years old. I am not what
you call fine & But all right.
I am five feet two. They call
me foxy brown,
                I like handsom
boys that play sports I wear
my black hair in a Bush.
I am very kind a like to talk,
I play around alot but I am
all right. And oh my name
is Rosaline Conesly. I am black.
I am knok needed. I like to
Bump.

Sample Profile

Questions came:

"That's a boy or girl name?"

"Why don't you write and find out?"

"Teacher, he's white or he's black?"

This black/white thing fascinated us. Remember, we had not required that they put their race on the profiles, and while some did so anyway, many did not. Once the question was posed, we all began listening to profiles with a new ear, looking for clues as to what that person's race might be. We discovered that there really *is* a "black sound":

"She white," someone would say. "White kids say 'great' — black kids say 'Dy-no-mite!' "

"She's black. Only black kids write stuff like 'I'm foxy and fine.' White kids don't say such boastful things about themselves in the profiles." To this same observation, however, the blacks countered, "White kids' profiles be *boring*; you don't learn nothin' about how they look from what they write!"

As each profile was read aloud, any students who wanted to write to that person raised their hands. If four hands went up, the profile went to the first hand raised, with instructions to pass it on to the next person, and then to numbers three and four.

As in the accelerated classes, our below-average students found much to deride. "How old you said these kids were?" or "That don't make *no* sense!" were refrains heard over and over. For nearly the first time ever, slow students were reading word for word what was actually written, if only so that they too could find a mistake to point out to the others. Once it was mentioned, however, that the kids in the other school might well be having the same reaction to *their* profiles, they suddenly started proofreading their letters *very* carefully. They started asking friends to read their letters before they were mailed, peering anxiously into their faces, looking for a response. And when later someone wrote, "I don't know if I want to keep writing to someone who's too lazy to look up the right spelling of the word *polka-dotted!*," that clinched it. The dictionary's popularity rose ten points.

A previously agreed-upon letter form was written on the board in both schools on the day profiles were read. Kids immediately started writing letters in answer to profiles, excited over the prospect of receiving an answer the very next day. Those who had forgotten their pencils wrung their hands, waiting for their friends to finish using theirs; those who forgot paper rushed to us for their handouts — but there simply wasn't enough to go around. Suddenly they realized the importance of being prepared; a lesson learned bitterly, for the mail went out that very afternoon.

Their friends, meanwhile, wrote five and six letters apiece. Letterboxes were set up and kids started pouring letters into the box on their way out

E. McMain School
5712 Colibene Ave.
New Orleans La 70125
Feb. 25, 1975

Mary Sterling
Period 6
Ms. Miller
Peter's Jr High School

Dear Mary
Hi! I heard you been
sick and I am sorry about that. I hope
you are feeling much better now.
My teacher said that you be absent
a lot is that true. I hope I never
get sick during the school days because
I don't want to miss any. I really
do love writing to the people at
Peter's Jr High School because they
all scund nice to me. Sorry the
letter so short. By now

Teresina Neapollioun
Period 6Th
MT Berlin
E McMain School

Response Letter

of class; by the day's end the letterbox overflowed. With so much mail, there was no point in waiting for the postal system. We became mailpersons, driving across town daily on an alternating basis. Daily delivery found kids running to their seats waiting for mail distribution, anxious lest they not hear their names called. Problems caused by absentees were handled with the courtesygram. This kept the lines of communication open, reassured the person waiting that he or she had not been overlooked or forgotten, and gave that person something tangible to hold when the mail was given out.

We had asked those who answered a profile to initial the back, so we could see which profiles hadn't been answered. Then we listed the unanswered profiles, and placed them atop the pack. Despite our precautions, some students received no mail that first week. We solved this temporarily by saying that perhaps the student who chose to write to them had been absent, and then passed the word to each other over the phone in the evenings, "Maria O., 6th period, hasn't gotten any letters. Was her profile misplaced?"

After the first week of the project, students started sending photographs of each other back and forth. Oh, the status of receiving a picture! The whole class gathered around the recipient. (One little boy snatched the picture he'd received to his bosom before anyone could get to him, and huddled in a corner, his back to the others — who swarmed all over him anyway!) The snapshots made their pen pals more real. Phone numbers were exchanged. The phone calls began, and simultaneously in both schools, the network began to move, "Can we have a picnic? Can we meet our pen pals? How? When? Where?"

By school bus, in the middle of a school day, at a centrally located neighborhood park, they met. Amid the laughter and shyness, with sandwiches and kickball, and dancing and clapping, there were questions and answers:

"We can have another picnic?"

"You bet."

"We can keep on writing till the end of school?"

"You bet."

Is this a great project? You bet!

E. McMain Secondary Magnet School
5712 South Clairborne Avenue
New Orleans, Louisiana 70125

April 8, _____ 1975

Rebecca Logan
Period I
Miss Muller
S. J. Peters School

Dear *Rebecca*,

Sherry Estay _____ is absent from school today, but when she returns she will get your letter dated *April 7,* 1975.

You do not have to answer this letter; it is a courtesy service provided by:

Charmaine Thompson
Period 6
Miss Berlin
E McMain School

Courtesygram

A Student Writers' Workshop

Zenobia Verner

*Seeing the students as resources for each other
can improve instruction in writing, according to
Zenobia Verner, editor,* English in Texas.

Amid outcries by college teachers, businessmen, and parents that today's young people can't write, and school teachers' outcries that students won't write, we hear two faint whispers. One whisper is from students who say, "Why write? For whom? Who needs it?" The other comes from a few persons who attempt to answer these questions, "To communicate your ideas and feelings to those who mean something to you."

Student Resources

We teachers like to say that we use every available resource in order to do our best job. But do we? Many of us fail to utilize the most valuable resource we have — students. Let us assume that your objective is to improve the quality of student writing — both what is said and how it is said. Let us also assume that you are determined not to play the game of making sure you have seen every error students have ever written so that you can penalize for each in assigning grades. With this in mind, how might you begin to use students as resources?

First, furnish them with sufficient writing experiences to give you several good samples for each. Then read each paper carefully to determine its best features. Read a second time to determine each student's most critical writing needs. On the basis of these readings, you can prepare an inventory of resources for students to use during writing workshop sessions. This inventory could consist of a chart listing under each writing area students who have expertise in that particular area. Be sure that every student is listed on the chart at least one time. You now have sufficient data to form writing workshop groups, each of which will have students with major writing strengths. For example, one group may consist of the following students: Susie, who is strong in spelling and punctuation but who needs help in paragraph development; Maria, who writes good paragraphs but needs help in verb tense; Benson, who presents ideas logically and creatively but has a spelling problem; Paul, who uses colorful words, has a

55

large vocabulary, and uses correct verb forms but needs help in punctuation; and Carrie Mae, who communicates her vivid imagination in her writing but needs help in subject-verb agreement.

Give each member of the group an editorial assignment. Point out to them that each member has at least one strength which other group members can rely on, and needs that others in the group can meet. Each group member, before turning in a paper to the teacher, must be sure to have at least one student editor in one of the areas previously identified by the teacher to read it and discuss suggestions for change. Usually students want to have more than one editor suggest changes in order to share their work with group members, and to have the paper as error-free as possible before turning it in.

Certainly you can't expect students to take a positive approach toward writing improvement unless you do. You can set the stage by (1) being sure you have pointed out strengths in each student's work; (2) emphasizing communication aspects of language, rather than social status aspects of language; (3) assuming a supportive (I'm OK; You're OK) role rather than a nonsupportive (I'm OK; You're not OK) role; and most importantly (4) making sure that students have the group skills to conduct a writers' workshop.

Successful group work is not accomplished by simply putting students in groups and giving them assignments. To insure successful group efforts to improve individual writing skills, spend some time getting the groups functioning and working together. Although frequently secondary teachers claim they don't have time to spend on such matters, the fact is that they don't have time not to. Techniques and resources for team building will not be addressed in this paper, for much is available in most professional libraries. Just be sure that before you attempt the writer's workshop activities suggested here, you involve these groups of students in activities which focus on: (1) building trust, (2) developing brainstorming techniques, (3) gaining skill in arriving at concensus, (4) assuming positive group roles, and (5) making group decisions. Even if students have had experience along these lines earlier in the semester or in other group situations, it is essential that they have these experiences in this new situation with these new group members to get them ready to focus on each other's writing as both audience and editor.

In addition, prepare a set of guidelines for your groups to follow in sharing and editing to insure their accomplishment of the writing outcomes which you and they consider important. Be sure they include suggestions and opportunities for group members to respond positively as an audience to each member's writing; to edit, discuss, revise, and discuss before papers are presented to the teacher or to other appropriate groups or individuals; and to check your inventory of essential writing skills whenever needed.

Newspaper Resources

Now let's set up some writing situations in which students can apply their group skills to share products of their writing and to edit for writing improvement. Rather than focus on paragraphing, verb forms, spelling, or punctuation for the entire class (for in any of these areas you have students who are quite capable), let's focus for illustrative purposes on another aspect of writing which can be of interest to everyone and which lends itself easily to a positive approach — point of view.

I suggest that the following activities be centered around the current day's newspaper rather than the literature anthology. This gives students an opportunity to work on material that is relevant to them and to begin with a not-so-difficult model as the literary masters. After students have experienced this type of activity for themselves, they may be ready to look at how literary masters handle point of view. A minimum of six current day's newspapers will be necessary to carry out the suggested activities (with each group using a separate section to complete one of the learning alternatives). More newspapers would provide opportunity for groups to have a wider selection from the following alternatives.

Ask one group to select a news story involving conflict between two or more persons. Each group member retells the story from the viewpoint of a different involved person such as: (1) the accused pusher, murderer, burglar, arsonist, etc.; (2) the policeman making the arrest; (3) a friend who was arrested with him; (4) the mother of the arrested man; (5) the father, brother, sister, grandparent of the accused; (6) another involved person whom the group identifies.

Another group of students may read the pet section of the classified ads. Each group member can choose one of the following viewpoints from which to write a story: (1) the pet; (2) the person who is advertising the pet for sale; (3) the person who considers buying; (4) another person or pet from either buyer or seller's household. Variations might include using a car, house, or some other item from the classified advertising section.

A third group might select a display ad and identify the audience to which it appeals. After the group has brainstormed possible appeals to new audiences, each group member can rewrite the ad for a different audience, such as school teachers, housewives, teenagers, builders, engineers, scientists, feminists, senior citizens, farmers, and so forth.

The next group may read Dear Abby or Ann Landers and select a specific letter. Each group member can write a second letter to Abby or Ann from the viewpoint of another person involved in the situation, such as a husband, wife, lover, mother, father, neighbor, son, daughter. Then students exchange letters and write Ann's or Abby's reply to another student's letter, or two groups could do this and exchange for writing replies.

Yet another group might respond to one of today's episodes in the comics from the viewpoint of different characters in the strip and then share their outcomes.

Another alternative would be for a group to respond to an editorial writer or other columnist from the viewpoint of different persons in the community.

It is essential for you and your students throughout the pre-writing, writing, editing, and sharing activities to keep in mind your objective — improvement of writing. Following such activities fewer students should be asking the questions, "Why write? For whom? Who needs it?"

They'd Rather Do It Themselves

Jeanine Rounds
Hawaii Curriculum Center
Honolulu, Hawaii

Several years ago, I decided to set myself the task of seeing if I could develop some kind of inductive approach for my expository writing course in which the students, high school juniors and seniors, would come to discover for themselves the "rules" about writing I had been expounding, and develop their own yardsticks for finding some of their own problems. Initially I questioned whether I would really be able to build such a curriculum, but the result has been far better than I had hoped.

One of the first activities is a thirty-minute writing sample. After I read these, they are filed in individual folders which are maintained by the student throughout the course. The contents are reviewed at each grading period.

During the next class meeting the students discuss, as informally as possible, what they hope to get out of the class. They usually tend to be quite ambitious in their goals and more demanding on themselves than I would be. I tell them I prefer not to put letter grades on their papers, but I promise to write lots of comments on the papers. If anybody is unhappy, I guarantee that if they come to me, I will give them a grade. The willingness to try the new approach is usually unanimous, and almost never does anyone come and request a grade on a paper.

Then the first assignment is given: the next time we meet we are going to retell *The Three Bears*! (Teachers can use anything they want for this task, but the students have fun with a story of this type.) Students might role-play the story from the point of view of Papa Bear relating the incident down at the corner bar, Mama Bear talking to the next-door nieghbor, Baby Bear telling his buddies, or Goldilocks telling her friends. We talk about the differences in the story as it is retold, and why these exist. Students especially notice the language changes and variance in details. Next we have Goldilocks retell the story to the police, at the parents' insistence. Again we examine the differences. By now the students have told *me* a great deal about the effects of changing audience and point of view. We have had considerable fun and, I hope, set the tone for the course.

The writing assignment that follows this exercise is three paragraphs: something that has happened to each student as told to a close friend, to a little-known older person, then as a parent would tell it. When students bring these papers to class, they meet in groups of four, read each other's paragraphs, and comment on the "realness" and effectiveness of the changes. They may choose one set to be read aloud. A general discussion follows about what they have observed.

The next writing assignment is to rewrite a familiar fairy tale as if they were one of the characters in the tale. Another activity may be to have the students rewrite the first paragraph of a given essay, directing it to a different and specific audience.

Students are now very familiar with the concepts of audience and point of view and their effects on writing; anything I might say about these topics would be redundant. There has been no need for me to expound on anything; they have told it all to me.

Next we study examples of contemporary music, films, etc. to help train students to recognize theses. Then I ask them to write several thesis sentences of their own, choose one, and write a paper. At this point I still have not "taught" the students anything explicitly about writing, or about any of the concepts we have covered. The exercise that follows the writing of this first real essay is one of the most important in this series. Each student is asked to "strip" his or her essay during a lab session in class. The stripping instructions are as follows:

1. Number each paragraph of your essay.
2. On a separate sheet of paper copy the one sentence in the essay that best sums up the main idea (the "thesis"), if there is one. If none, write NONE.
3. Now check each paragraph and see if you can find one sentence which sums up the ideas of the paragraph, a sort of topic sentence.

4. On the separate paper, opposite the number which corresponds to each paragraph, write the sentence you found. If you find none, write NONE. If you discover your paragraph has more than one main idea, write all of them down.
5. Check the sentences on the separate paper and see if they follow in some sort of logical sequence.
6. Check the rest of the sentences in each paragraph to see if they develop the topic idea.
7. Now see me for conference.

This is always an exciting class. Comments and exclamations emanate from all sides of the room as the students are forced to look at their own writing "stripped" down to its bare bones; some of them see they have the ankle bone connected to the neck bone. "Wow! What a mess this is!" "*Now* I see why it didn't sound right!" "*Why* didn't anybody tell me this before!" The important point is that their attention is directed to their own writing in a very novel way. The teacher need not make one observation or criticism; they see for themselves where the organizational problems lie. During the individual conferences that follow, the students map out their own revisions, based on the construction problems they themselves have observed.

Magazine Writers in the Junior High: The Publishing Game

John Hollowell

Making writing class a "real-world" situation with audience clearly established proved successful in the junior high school classes of John Hollowell, presently teaching English at the University of Arizona in Tucson.

"The Publishing Game," a simulation game designed for use in the junior high, mirrors the real-world process of writing and editing a small magazine.[1] Students no longer write essays for the teacher's red pencil, but are miraculously transformed into writers, poets, reviewers, and editors of a magazine staff. The game format, or role-playing, accomplishes two important things: (1) the valid purpose of writing for an audience is established, and (2) reading, writing, editing and proofreading are combined into a coherent pattern which culminates in a tangible product — a class magazine.

Organizing the Game

Step I: Divide the class into teams (publishing companies) of about 10-15 students each.

Step II: The teacher (who plays publisher) kicks off the game with an introductory speech that provides the context for play and tells students about their roles in the game.

PUBLISHER'S SPEECH
(gruffly)

"The publishing game is a tough business. Frankly, I've been discouraged by our recent sales record. We're in a big slump! To turn the tide of this economic disaster, I'm going to ask each publishing company to create a magazine on the theme of Spring (substitute any thematic idea). Each company will write the stories and articles for the magazine by doing the special jobs in these JOB PACKETS (8½" x 11" envelopes). Everything you must do is included on your instruction sheets

---

[1] An initial version of "The Publishing Game" was developed with the help of Mr. Gene Templeton and Mr. Larry Schwartz in a graduate methods seminar at the University of Michigan under the direction of Professor Stephen Dunning.

in the packets, but as your publisher, I'll be around to help out and answer questions. The first thing you will do is hold a meeting of your company to decide on the name of the magazine and the name of your company. But let's stop all this jawing and roll the presses. May the best team, er, company, win!" (*Enthusiastically hand out job packets to each team.*)

Step III: Each job packet is carefully prepared in advance by the teacher. The key to the simulation is that the instructions for writing, writing samples, colorful magazine pictures, and any other materials are included in 8½" x 11" envelopes.

Description of Job Packets

While space does not allow for a full description of each job, the following examples of job packets are illustrative of the variety of writing tasks I have used successfully.

PACKET 1: Format Editor. You're the quarterback of your team! It's up to you to decide how the various parts of the magazine will be put together. Find out from all other staff members what articles they are working on, then make a list of the titles and lengths. Look over shoulders, ask questions, bug people to do their jobs!

Specific Jobs: (1) Make a table of contents of all articles, poems, and stories for the magazine. Assign page numbers to each entry.

(2) Next, make a copyright page for the magazine using one from a book or magazine as an example. Be sure to include the facts of publication, the name of the company, and the date.

(3) Proofread all the work turned in to you. Correct grammar, spelling, and other errors. (Writers who finish early should help you with this job.)

PACKET 2: Biography Editor (assign two students, if desired). This editor writes a 40-50 word "Contributor's Note" for each of the writers, poets, and editors on the team. His specific task is to interview each team member to find out hometown and main interests, previous publications, and facts about personal life. (Writers should be encouraged to "make up" their backgrounds as much as they want.) A sample biographical entry is included in the packet:

JOHN DOE is a contributing editor to_____(name of magazine)_____. His stories have appeared in *Mad* magazine and in *Scholastic Scope.* His latest venture is the founding of a new journal on the popular arts, *The Coyote Review.* John is a bachelor and lives in Yuma, Arizona, with his pet beagle, Lucky.

PACKET 3: Review Editor. This editor writes reviews (like dust jacket blurbs) for the back cover of the magazine. The editor may select excerpts of quotations from the sample blurbs included in the packet or write phony reviews of his own. His instructions read:

> Select the best quotations from the sample reviews that show your company's magazine in the best light. Choose a few sentences from each review which point out the best qualities of your magazine. Or, better yet, make up some of your own.

Four or five sample reviews are included in the packet as models, such as:

> "Groovy! Outasite! Far out! That's the only way I can describe _____(name of magazine)_____. These young dudes can really write, man. Can you dig it? So drop all those other books about birds singing and spring, and pick up on_____(repeat name)_____. For a fast-moving anthology of stories and verse — this is it."
>
> *— Rolling Stone*

PACKETS 4-8: Writers. (Any number of writer packets can be created depending upon the size of the teams. Also, if desired, more than one student can be assigned to the same packet. The tasks listed are suggestive of what might be required.)

Writer #1: Instructions and materials included in the packet are as follows:

(1) Three to five bright, colorful magazine pictures depicting people in action scenes related to the theme of the issue.

(2) Instructions for writing a particular prose or verse form. Usually a specified word count or length is helpful to students.

(3) A model of the kind of writing required. For example, writers might be asked to create cinquains, haiku, or narrative paragraphs about the subjects of the photographs in the packet.

For example: Write a cinquain about the Spring scene in your favorite photograph in the packet.

Cinquain Rules	*Sample Cinquain*
line 1 — noun, one word	Dove,
line 2 — 2 words, describing noun in line 1	White, soaring
line 3 — 3 words, showing action of noun in line 1	Wings flapping, stirring
line 4 — 4 words, showing your feelings or thoughts about noun in line 1	My heart lifts up
line 5 — 1 word, a synonym for noun in line 1	Bird

PACKET 9: Promotion Editor. This writer creates a three-minute speech calculated to "sell" the company's magazine to potential buyers (students in other classes?). The instructions read:

(1) Make your talk as persuasive as possible. To do so, you will need to find out specific information, such as: (a) the titles and writers for each story, poem, and article; (b) the title and price of the magazine; and (c) biographical information about the writers and editors on the staff (see the Biography Editor).

(2) Now write out a rough draft of your speech. Be sure to consider the strong points of your publication and the kinds of people who may want to buy it — your audience!

(3) When the magazine is put together, you will deliver your talk before the entire group.

(As an added gimmick, sample order forms might be dittoed off and placed in the packet for the Promotion Editor to distribute.)

PACKET 10: Poetry Editor. Three short poems related to the theme of the magazine are included in the packet. For our issue on Spring, we chose E. E. Cummings' "In Just Spring," Frost's "Spring Pools," and Millay's "Spring." This editor's instructions read:

(1) Read each of the three poems slowly and carefully. Which one do you like best? Why? Be sure to consider the poet's use of language and his specific images. Which poem makes you *see* Spring most clearly in your mind?

(2) Write a 25-30 word introduction for the poem. Discuss some of the things you like about the poem and introduce it to a reader. This brief introduction is called a HEADNOTE.

(3) If you have time, do the same thing for another of the poems in your packet, or find a similar poem in a magazine or book.

Step IV: When each student has completed his or her writing task and has turned in the finished product to the Format Editor, papers should be exchanged among the team members for proofreading and correction of errors. The game context provides good incentive for working on these skills. Last, finished copies of all materials are written out neatly and decorative covers for the magazines may be designed. Scissors, magic markers, crayons, and construction paper should be available at this point.

Fortunately, there need not be "winners" and "losers" in this game. The Publisher has the option of choosing the best magazine, or students may vote to determine the winner. The best team, if desired, can be rewarded with points, praise, or grades. Better yet, the magazines can be displayed prominently in the classroom, "published" on dittoes, or placed in the school library.

Outcomes

The responses of the junior high classes I have worked with, and those of my student teachers, have been enthusiastic. Students find the writing jobs fun. A former student teacher wrote recently, "I got some really fantastic work. I was shocked (and they were, too) to see that they could write so well." "The Publishing Game," like other role-playing or gaming experiences, motivates powerfully because it parallels the reasons professional writers write — to be read. Its chief assets are that the activities create a sense of cooperation among students of differing abilities, that students are given a context in which editing and proofreading make sense, and finally, that the teacher can surrender his or her red pencil to become an adviser and a resource rather than a mere giver of grades.

Writing about Smiles and Other Human Processes

Lucky Jacobs
University of Virginia

Models, coupled with student activities, can provide a means for eliciting personal writing. The model, whether it be poem, paragraph, or journal excerpt, should bring students back into the real world of their own human processes. A concrete example:

Elevator Connection

Lucky Jacobs

Seeing the girl who stands all alone
in the elevator is more than he can stand.
For fourteen of the twenty floors
the silence is unbearable.
"Really slow" he says.
She smiles,
a smile somewhere between
"yes" and "how obvious."
"I'm going to the nineteenth floor"
he says.
She smiles,
a smile somewhere between
"how obvious" and "what a coincidence,
small world, married? I'm going to
the seventeenth."

You might have the students practice connotative smiles on each other. Ask them to describe each other's smiles: aggressive — teeth bared like a wolf; arrogant — know it all; open — come on in and chat with me; coy; tension-relieving; etc. Students could role-play some settings where different kinds of smiles occur. Have them try writing about a particular kind of smile in a particular setting.

Myth-making, another ancient human process, is a natural activity for students from eight to eighty. A good model is Kenneth Patchen's poem "The Origin of Baseball." Ask your students to tell some daffy myths about the origins of things, e.g., hair, elephants, ceilings, greeting, smiling, running, etc. I think you will find that your students can do this quite well.

A third human process approach centers around "time-wasting." You might want to tell students some of your favorite ways of wasting time. Be quirky. Try to slip in some things which, from a strictly pragmatic point of view, might seem like a waste of time, but from a deeper point of view might seem important. Ask the students for some of their favorite time-wasting activities. A concrete phenomenological discussion of values with respect to "time-wasting" should occur. For example: is it a waste of time when you go fishing and do not catch a "real" fish? A good model poem here is Robert Bly's "Driving to Town Late to Mail a Letter." Ask the students to write about some things that they do to waste time. Images of particular places, activities, and settings should be leaping into their minds by now.

Some further examples of human processes for writing:
1. Greeting or taking leave
2. Envying
3. Things you would like to remember; things you would like to forget
4. Wearing a mask

The exciting classroom question becomes: What kinds of things do human beings predicate in what kinds of settings? The written responses will not focus on vague abstraction, nor on previously held opinion, but rather on the fabulous realities of personal experience. When students share these experiences, magical things happen.

Sharpening Technique

Exploration with Language

Victor Froese

A series of experiments can focus children's attention on language in ways that assist oral and written communication. Victor Froese is an assistant professor at the University of Manitoba, Winnipeg, Canada.

Most students see the study of language as a series of exercises on nouns and verbs, *can* versus *may*, and other equally dull aspects of grammar. It is important to make them realize that language can be exciting. It is, in fact, a science that can be explored through experimentation to reveal *how* we use language to communicate and understand, *how* we use language to remember things, and *how* language changes.

The following experiments, addressed to the student, can show ways in which oral and written language are different.

Exploration 1

Divide into groups of 4 or 5 students. Take the words below and try to say them in as many different ways as possible. Make a question out of them, then make a commmand, and so on.

SENTENCE: What is this thing called John?

Now write down all the different versions. How can you show that they are said differently? After about ten minutes share the findings of your group with the other groups. Make a list of the differences between the oral and written forms of this sentence. Try to answer these questions:

  a. When you talk, how do you get the information that punctuation shows in writing? (Say some questions and commands out loud and listen carefully.)
  b. Are there clues to meaning when using oral language that are not part of the sentence? (Watch the person's face, hands, etc.) Try saying one of the sentences in a sarcastic way.
  c. Is oral or written language clearer in getting a message across? Explain your answer.

Another way to look at differences in oral and written language is to look at words that can cause difficulties in oral language but rarely do in

written form. There are at least two labels for these words:
1. Homonyms — reed, rēad
2. Homographs — read, rĕad

You can be a word detective and try to figure out what these labels mean. Here are some clues:

homo means *same or similar* (as in homogenize)

graph means something *drawn or written* (as in monograph)

onym means *word or name* (as in acronym)

Additional clue: In this case *onym* refers to the sound of the word.

Now use a dictionary to compare the meanings. If you want to make it a real challenge add "homophones" to your list.

After you are sure of the meaning, especially of the term *homonym*, try the next experiment.

Exploration 2

Here is a sentence which could contain either of two or three homonyms but does not give any clues to their meanings. Your task is to ask the question of someone else and to see which and how many meanings he or she gives you. The extra words are put in for your benefit: don't give any clues to the person you are working with. Someone outside your class might be the best to interview, perhaps your parents.

a. What does quarts mean?
   quartz

b. What does break mean?
   brake

c. What does rays mean?
   raise
   raze

d. What does rain mean?
   rein
   reign

Try to come to some conclusions about your findings:
a. Did you get more meanings from older students?
b. Were you often asked: "Which word or spelling do you mean?"
c. Why are the questions you asked actually unclear?
d. Why don't you ordinarly have difficulty in telling which one of two or three homonyms is meant? Is it different for oral and written language?

Here is a third way in which you can learn some differences between oral and written language. For this experiment it is best to have a tape recorder since you will want to listen to how you explained the experiment to someone else. (If you have several recorders, groups could be used.)

Exploration 3

One way to do this experiment is to work in pairs. That is, *one* person of each pair will study the directions for the game called "Mill" so that he or she can explain the game to the partner. The other person may construct a game board and chips with which to play the game. Five to ten minutes should be enough time to prepare.

Then each person who has studied the rules explains the game to his or her partner. One or more of these explanations should be recorded for further study. A group of students may wish to transcribe (write out what the person said) one of the explanations.

Rules for "The Mill"

Equipment: Make a playing board similar to the one in the picture from 9″ x 9″ construction paper. You will also need two sets of nine chips about ½″ x ½″. Each set of chips could be cut from different colored construction paper.

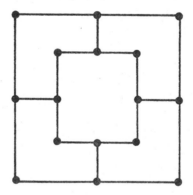

Instructions: Each player in turn places a chip on any empty dot until all the chips are put down. A chip may then be moved along any line to the next empty dot. The object, both in putting chips on the board and in moving them, is to arrange three chips of one's own color in a row. Such a row is called a *mill*. When you have completed a mill you may remove any one of the opponent's chips as long as it is not part of a closed or complete mill. Once chips are removed from the board they may not be used again. Three more rules must be remembered: (1) A chip that is part of a closed or complete mill cannot be removed; (2) You may open and close a mill as many times as you want to by moving any one of the chips but when it is open the pieces may be removed by the opponent completing a mill (only a closed mill is safe); (3) A player who cannot move or who has only two pieces left, loses.

Now listen to the tape again or look at a transcription (a written out version of the tape) and try to answer these questions:
a. What did you notice about the overall length of the description compared to the written rules?
b. What kinds of words or expressions did you hear on the tape which are not found in the written rules?
c. Which was easier to understand for you, the written or the oral form of the game? Explain or compare.
d. What are some of the most important differences between the written and the oral forms of the rules?
Are these differences also true for other kinds of oral and written language?

We have already discovered some differences between oral and written language. However, there are actually more similarities. For example, you have the ability to make up completely original sentences — you have not learned these sentences but you have learned how to put them together. *Linguists often think about this ability as a set of rules.*
NOTE: You can understand this sentence quite well but you have *never* seen it before! You would also find it extremely difficult to find an identical sentence anywhere (except in another copy of the same book).

The rules which you have learned are not easy to describe; in fact, you probably cannot explain them or are not aware of knowing them. But they are quite useful. Here is a chance to use them.

Arrange these words in the way you think they should go:
a, ball, big, he, red, saw

Now compare what you wrote with others in the class. Can you explain your finding? Did anyone have the word *red* before the word *big*?

Your rules also help you tell a good sentence from a poor sentence or from strings of words which are not sentences at all. Try these.

	good sentence	poor sentence	not a sentence
They saw a flower purple.	( )	( )	( )
One of them saw a walking.	( )	( )	( )
Everybody needs milk.	( )	( )	( )
All nobody does cleverly was.	( )	( )	( )

You may also have strings of words that look like sentences but don't make sense. For example: One of them saw a flour. You can do an experiment to learn more about your language using a rather famous poem.

'Twas° brillig, and the slithy toves
Did gyre and gimble in the wabe:
All mimsy were the borogroves,
And the mome raths outgrabe.

(°'*Twas* is shortened from *it was.*)

Exploration 4

Write out this poem on some paper. Then (1) underline all the "real" words. Now (2) circle all the nonsense words which are "things." (3) Draw boxes around "action" words. (4) Draw wiggly lines under "describing" words. (5) Write the poem out again keeping only the real words and leaving a blank for each nonsense word (make a line to indicate each missing word). Now make up your own poem by filling in real words where you left the blanks before. (6) For fun look up *Through the Looking Glass* by Lewis Carroll. In that story Humpty Dumpty explains the "nonsense" words in the poem. This poem is over 100 years old!

Your knowledge of your language made it possible for you to select words which we called either "real," "nonsense," "action," "describing," or "thing" words.

Most of the "real" words in the poem are small words which have little meaning as compared to "thing," "action," or "describing" words. (1) Compare the number of "real" words to the number of "nonsense" words. (2) Count the number of small words such as *on, a, as, by, the, an, in, to, from, of* in the following passage. What part of all the words in the passage are these small words?

On a bright day the children in the
town of Summerville who travelled to school
disappeared from the face of the earth. It
seemed as if they had been sucked up by an
interplanetary vacuum.

(3) Look at other sentences and passages to see how many of these kinds of words they contain. How important are these little words?

In written language, a system of punctuation marks has been developed. This system corresponds to the way you change your voice, or the way you emphasize certain words, or the way your voice stops briefly between some words or groups of words.

Exploration 5

It is not always easy to hear what kind of punctuation would be used if the sentence were written. Not all punctuation marks are always represented by the same change in sound either. But most of the time you can tell which mark is intended. Read these sentences to a friend and ask what kind of punctuation he or she thinks is in the sentence.

a. Are you playing?
b. Jump!
c. That is a ball.
d. Tom, the pitcher is ready.
e. The bat, the ball, and the glove were lost.
f. Did you find them? (*Note*: Begin this sentence and (a) with *where* or *why* and it becomes more difficult to hear the "punctuation" intended.)
g. Put the plate back.
h. Wow, is that a slam!

What was your partner's score? Together with your partner try to explain how you can tell the differences.

Writing the words you hear can be a real problem! Read this poem and discuss some of the problems.

ENGLISH

I take it you already know
Of tough and bough and cough and dough?
Others may stumble, but not you
On hiccough, thorough, slough and through?
Well done! And now you wish, perhaps,
To learn of less familiar traps?

Beware of heard, a dreadful word
That looks like beard and sounds like bird,
And dead: it's said like bed, not bead —
For goodness sake, don't call it deed!
Watch out for meat and great and threat,
(They rhyme with suite and straight and debt.)
A moth is not a moth in mother
Nor both in bother, broth in brother,

And here is not a match for there,
And dear and fear for bear and pear,
And then there's dose and rose and lose —
Just look them up — and goose and choose,
And cork and work and card and ward,
And font and front and word and sword,
And do and go, and thwart and cart —
Come, come, I've hardly made a start!

A dreadful language? Why, man alive!
I'd learned to talk it when I was five,
And yet to write it, the more I tried,
I hadn't learned it at fifty-five.

Author unknown

Our peculiar spellings are partly due to the fact that we have borrowed many of our words from other languages. Can you name some? Over the years our pronunciations of words have also changed. For example "mouse" was pronounced like "moose" by the Normans.

Many words that rhyme are also spelled quite differently — choir, higher, yacht, not.

Some people have suggested that we should write all words the way they sound. This sounds like a good idea but it actually would require you to learn even more spellings. Instead of *do* and *does* (which look somewhat alike) you might have *doo* and *duz* (which don't look alike). How might these words change in spelling?

soft — sof*t*en

cour*a*ge — cour*a*geous

medi*c*ine — medi*c*al

Make a collection of words spelled in unusual ways and post them on the bulletin board.

Exploration 6

Construct a game using words from the poem "English." You may wish to add other words to your game as well. Make a board from construction paper containing the various sounds:

12 inches

	gh sounds like f	*gh* is silent	other *gh* sounds
9 inches	*ea* sounds like ē	*ea* sounds like â	other *ea* sounds

Next, write words containing the *gh* and *ea* sounds on 3″ cards. You may win the game by sorting the cards the fastest or by the number of cards correctly placed. Make other games like it by using different letter combinations.

I Swapped Words for Stories

R. Baird Shuman

*A group of low track students disproved the
assumption that they were incapable of writing
poetry. R. Baird Shuman is professor of education
at Duke University, Durham, North Carolina.*

My writing workshop was essentially designed to help above average senior high school students write poetry. But when I arrived at the school to spend a week as writer-in-residence, I asked to be permitted to work with at least one very slow class. My hosts were dubious; I was insistent. The slowest tenth grade English class met during the sixth period, the last period of the day. Twenty-two youngsters, most of them boys, had reached a truce with the teacher. If he would not hassle them, they would not hassle him.

My visit, an expensive one for the school district, had been well publicized. Everyone in the small town in which the high school was situated knew that a poet was being brought in for a week, that some ordinary kids from the town might be turned into poets. They had all seen *The Waltons* and cherished the idea that a John Boy might be lurking in the house next door or around the corner or down the street.

No one had expected that the visitor would work with the 09s, as the slow learners were euphemistically labeled. Least of all did the 09s expect to be included in the much touted literary activities of *Poetry Week*. Therefore, when I appeared in their class the first day and was introduced, they looked puzzled.

I had tried to anticipate some of the problems I might meet with these students. On a practical level, I expected that few of them would have pens or pencils and paper. I overcame the latter difficulty by passing out a sheet of paper to everyone. I said that everyone should take out a pen or pencil; and when a chorus admitted to having neither, I cooly produced a handful of freshly sharpened pencils that I had prepared for the occasion. I asked Lenny, a boy who walked with a swagger and wore his hat in class, to hand them out, to remember who had them, and to make sure that we got them all back.

Again on a practical level, I had anticipated that some of the students probably could not read or write sufficiently well to function in a situation involving independent writing activities. I sought to overcome this by announcing quite simply, "Some of us work better together, others better alone. We are going to be doing some writing, so if you want to work with one or more other people, that's fine. If you are more comfortable working alone, that's fine, too. It's a free country! But if you are in a group, make sure that everyone's name gets on whatever you write to turn in." Having said this, I told them to move into groups if that was the way they preferred to write. Most of them chose to work with one or more other students.

On the creative level, I knew that the exercise had to be structured. Realistically these students could not just be asked to write freely nor could they at this point be given a literary topic to write about. I could not at this stage expect success if I plunged them right into poetry writing — although before the week was over, they *were* writing poetry.

Since I had had little time to prepare anything elaborate, I announced, "We're going to make a swap. I'll give you some words and you give me a story. All of the words I give you should appear somewhere in your story." The words I used on that particular day were *approximate, estimated, fortunately, investigation, lurked, motivated, patrolling, revenge, suspicion,* and *tampered.*

The list of words did not come from a vocabulary list or from a spelling list, but rather were the ten most difficult words in a front page newspaper story from the county paper — a weekly — which had been delivered to the school library, hot off the presses, during fourth period lunch. It told of a mountain feud, well known to all of the students, which had resulted in a shooting the week before.

Given this assignment, the students balked at the difficulty of the words. But those working in groups found that nearly everyone in the group knew some of the words — although not all could read them — and I circulated, helping them with words they were stuck on, mostly having them sound the problem words out, after which I used them in a sentence, and had the students guess at meaning through contextual clues. At that point, when the kids were new to me and I to them, I thought it best not to burden them with running to the dictionary, a task which is very time-consuming for the disabled reader.

The students worked for about twenty minutes, all in a very spirited manner, before I handed out to them a dittoed reproduction of the story, put on a ditto master by photographic process so that it looked exactly as it had in the county paper. After we had read the news story, they began to read what they had done with the words I had given them, swapping their stories for my words, as it were.

By the next day, I had dittoed all of their stories, complete and incomplete, and revision groups began working on stories other than those they had worked on the preceding day. We proceeded from that to writing dialogues based on newspaper stories; before the week was out, some of the students were writing poetry, sometimes based on incidents in news stories, sometimes just using some of the words they had found in the newspaper.

By mid-week I had the students doing careful revisions and copying these revisions onto ditto masters, using ballpoint pens. I encouraged illustrations, and I posted student work all over the school. Perhaps it is significant that when we entered this stage, everyone remembered to bring their own pen and paper. And at about this stage, Lenny removed his hat, an adornment which he was said to have worn to class since September.

"To Be" or Not "To Be": Let the Reader Decide

Randell Shutt

A challenge to avoid "to be" forms made students aware of ways to give life to their writing. Randell Shutt teaches at Northern Arizona University, Flagstaff, Arizona.

As you read, please note that I carefully avoid all use of "to be" in its identification or predication forms. Why? Because in my English Composition course, I try to train students to avoid "to be" forms in their writing, and I feel pushed to provide a model.

Ever since Alfred Korzybski probed the principle of "Non-Identity," embracers of this concept have popularized it and applied it to human behavior. Some of the early popularizers include S. I. Hayakawa, Wendell Johnson and Irving Lee. More recently, the "Is of Identity Test," developed by Thomas M. Weiss, measures degree of social adjustment. D. David Bourland, Jr. has adopted a new form of English he calls E-Prime (English without "to be"). And Don Fabun, Publications Editor in the Public Affairs Department of Kaiser Aluminum and Chemical Corporation, brought the problem of "is" to the attention of the business world. All of these scholars reiterate the basic idea that the English language structure with its predominance of "to be" forms encourages the native English speaker to misevaluate the process nature of the nonverbal world.

In my English classes, the students have doubts when I suggest that two-thirds of their so-called verbs never jump off the page or image any action for the reader; they just lie on the page, static and frozen. But when the students actually count their is, was, am, are, were, and will be structures, they discover that my statement accurately describes three-fourths of their writing.

My procedure for remedying the "to be" syndrome takes the following form. First I guarantee the students that if they adopt my suggestion, the quality of their writing will improve dramatically. Interest immediately mounts, although some students continue to look skeptical. Then I present a twenty-minute lecturette on the lack of correspondence between the static nature of "to be" statements and the dynamic nature of the nonverbal

78

"operational" world. The students pay close attention, partly because I tell them ahead of time that I will only talk twenty minutes, and partly because I warn them that they will have to make practical application of this principle.

After the lecturette and the short question and answer session, I divide the class into groups of three and hand each group a 3 x 5 card with an "is of identity" or an "is of predication" statement written on the card. Examples of some of these statements are:

1. She *is* a good student.
2. She *is* a bad driver.
3. I *am* the silent type.
4. He *is* an Italian.
5. Mr. Jones *is* rich.
6. She *is* a sorority girl.
7. My boyfriend *is* the most wonderful man in the world.
8. He *is* patriotic.
9. People over thirty *are* weird.
10. He *is* a good Catholic.

Then I usually demonstrate by putting a sentence on the board and saying. "I will make a list of personal, observable statements that might lead me to the eventual statement: 'The school cafeteria food *is* lousy.'" Then I list three or four criteria like:

1. The cooks serve mystery meat on Monday, Tuesday, and Wednesday.
2. By the end of the week, the lettuce sags.
3. I needed a jack hammer to puncture the baked potato last Friday.
4. The vanilla, butterscotch and chocolate puddings taste like white, tan and brown glue.

I try to think of humorous, yet vivid kinds of statements that will encourage a little enthusiasm and creativity.

Then I turn them loose to create their own personal list of criteria for the particular statement that I handed to the group. After ten or fifteen minutes, I suggest that the individuals in each group compare lists, agree on the most effective statements and read them aloud to the class.

A sampling of student responses to this exercise might help to show some of the benefits of writing without "to be." Some statements on personal lists of criteria that developed from "She *is* a good student" revealed:

She pours over the books five hours every night.
She dreams about math problems.
She explains to other students who do not understand.
She talks in class rather than sitting like a Zombie.
She turns in her assignments on time.

Statements resulting from "She *is* a bad driver" disclosed:

> She ran six stop signs last week.
> She pumps the gas pedal too much.
> She doesn't use her turn signals.
> She drinks while she drives.
> She watches pedestrians instead of the road.
> Officer Goodman gave her 12 speeding tickets last month.
> I saw her make a U-turn on a hill.
> She hit a fire hydrant yesterday with her car.

Statements resulting from "I *am* the silent type" produced:

> I stutter when I talk to anyone.
> I bite my fingernails when asked a question.
> I play solitaire in the evenings.
> I never raise my hand to answer in class.
> I like to walk alone.
> I blush when someone speaks to me.
> I usually eat alone.
> I sit in the back of the class.
> I meditate for an hour each day.

The students quickly realize that when they substitute statements that show people acting, doing, or operating, for statements that identify or predicate, their writing begins to move. With practice it begins to sparkle a little. Some of them even realize that they pay their reader the courtesy of letting him devise his own predictions from their statements based on observation rather than "freezing" the reader into the writer's attitude. For example, the *reader* can decide whether "People over thirty *are* weird" after reading about their observable behavior.

Another benefit that, to me at least, appears far more long-reaching than improved writing IS that the students start paying attention to the experience which precedes the words that describe the experience. In Korzybski's terms, they become extensionally oriented rather than intensionally oriented; they become "fact" minded rather than "word" minded. I believe that this kind of awareness may stay with them long after they have "taken" my class.

References

> Korzybski, Alfred. *Science and Sanity: An Introduction to Non-Aristotelian Systems and General Semantics.* Lakeville, Conn.: International Non-Aristotelian Library Publishing Co., 1933.
> Hayakawa, S. I. *Language in Thought and Action.* New York: Harcourt, Brace & World, 1939.
> Johnson, Wendell. *People in Quandries: The Semantics of Personal Adjustment.* New York: Harper & Row, 1945.

Lee, Irving. *Language Habits in Human Affairs: An Introduction to General Semantics.* New York: Harper & Row, 1941.

Weiss, Thomas M. *The "Is of Identity" Test.* San Francisco: International Society for General Semantics, 1954.

Bourland, D. David, Jr. "The Un-Isness of Is." *Time,* 23 May 1969.

Fabun, Don. "The Trouble with Is, Is Is." *Communications: The Transfer of Meaning.* Beverly Hills, Calif.: Glencoe Press, 1968.

Writing in Groups

Beverly Haley
Fort Morgan High School
Fort Morgan, Colorado

Writing in groups is successful in a variety of ways for developing student writing skills. This technic can work for students of any age, any ability, or any level of interest. Design the writing assignment according to the group with which you're working and in connection with something the class has been studying or that you want to introduce.

Divide students into groups of three or four. I like to assign the group members to include both sexes, students not belonging to the same "clique," students of different personality and leadership types. The "mixing" creates a situation in which the students learn to know and respect one another and to pool their abilities.

The kinds of assignments I have tried are intended to make the students aware of the various elements in a story — setting, characters, conflict, plot — and what role each element will play. But more than this, the assignments sharpen student awareness of writing *style*: who is going to tell the story and how would this particular narrator tell it? what language would he or she use? what figures of speech? tone? what point in the action would the narrator select as the starting point? how would the narrator end it?

This is usually a three-class-period assignment. The first day is for discussing and deciding on the approach — tossing ideas around, seeing what the alternatives are, then making a group decision. The second day the groups may be able to finish a rough draft. The third day is for any finishing up, rewriting, and getting the product into its final form.

1. Write the plot outline of a story on the blackboard (for example, the plot of Liam O'Flaherty's "The Sniper," or make up a plot line of your own). Then each group simply "fills out" the story deciding who the narrator will be, what tone to adopt, and the type of diction to use. If you use a published story, try to pick one you think the students may not have read. After the group stories have all been heard, read the professional's story.

It is not unusual to have a student-written story turn out to be as good as or better than the professional's.

2. After your class has studied several authors of widely varied writing styles, assign each group to *be* one of the authors (e.g., Group A is Hemingway, Group B is Hawthorne, Group C is Steinbeck). Each student is given a copy of "The Little Red Hen" (or other familiar children's tale). Each group then rewrites the story in the style of the assigned author.

Take a familiar fable (distribute dittoed copies again as in #2) and have each group rewrite the fable from different points of view (a 19th-century Texas cowboy, a New England teacher, a 21st-century astronaut, etc.).

Besides getting to know each other better and learning to work together, students doing group writing learn to "brainstorm" and to see how one idea leads to another. They discuss how to organize and how to make transitions. They weigh the advantages and disadvantages of adopting a particular point of view and a particular writing style. They have the fun and pride of creating something together, and they develop a real feel for the writing process and an appreciation for the skill of the writer.

Of Newspapers and Student Writing

Richard E. Barbieri

Using the newspaper as a writing model helped students improve their writing. Richard E. Barbieri teaches English at Milton Academy, Milton, Massachusetts.

Every spring for three years our juniors took a six-week writing workshop between their final exams and the year's end. (This period, originally designed to give seniors an opportunity for independent projects, has also allowed us to experiment with new curricula for other classes.) The workshop was heavily oriented toward the use of writing models, with examples ranging from Macaulay and Carlyle to Joan Didion and Pauline Kael. When, in the course's third year, teachers were given the opportunity to devise their own syllabuses instead of following a departmental format, I chose to use our local newspaper, the *Boston Globe*, as a text. I had long thought of giving such a course, but its ultimate success, I believe, was due in about equal parts to prior planning and to unforeseen opportunities presented by the events of the term.

The newspaper seemed a logical writing model for several reasons. First, I wished to avoid the tyranny of purely literary examples. I felt that students who were baffled by the command to write like Bacon, Ruskin, or Orwell might find authors of lesser stature less daunting. Further, as I explained to the class in our first meeting, daily newspaper writers were not only closer to them in ability than the great essayists, but shared with students restrictions of time and space in the writing of their essays. Few students have the staying power to write their own *Modest Proposal* in anything approaching Swift's length, and none have the time to do so between the time a paper is assigned and the due date. Giving the novice the same amount of time as the columnist to produce an essay of similar scope gives him or her a better chance of creating something which will satisfy the hopes and expectations of both writer and reader. Finally, it was my hope that the immediacy, the "relevance" if we must, of newspaper subject matter, together with its variety, would keep enthusiasm from ebbing over six weeks of writing.

These premises seemed justified during the first few weeks of the term as we learned our way around the paper, concentrating most heavily on the op-ed page and the various columnists scattered through the paper's second section. Students began by writing a direct imitation of their favorite column from the first day's op-ed page, and we compared observations. As often as possible I shared assignments with the class, working under a pseudonym, as did they, and gained the pleasure of turning out at least one pretty fair Art Buchwald imitation. We went on to discuss what was distinctive about each author's style, outlook, etc., as well as what seemed to be the distinctive characteristics of good newspaper writing in general. We found ourselves particularly interested in noting how different writers began their columns; few if any followed the automatic sort of "in this paper I will" format, inculcated by strict, outline-fixated constructionists, which makes so many student papers so immediately uninviting.

We also agreed that the best columnists (I think particularly here of nationally syndicated columnists like Mike Royko, and of local observer Diane White) excelled at moving from the particular to the general, or at remaining vividly in the dramatically observed incident while nevertheless making a broadly applicable point. One column by Ms. White, for example, described the shock of encountering an elderly woman on the street and slowly realizing that the lady's bag of dog food was meant for herself and not for a pet. Pieces like this did far more than any exhortation could to convince students of the value of being specific and observing closely when writing about "urban poverty" or "old age in America." Subsequent essays, in which students were asked to follow a similar format in describing a chance encounter and the reflections occasioned by it, were noticeably more vivid, and more logically developed as well.

We were moving at a rapid pace and soon found it impossible to keep up with all the new and interesting possibilities suggested by each day's paper. Even skipping a day or two's issues left us all we could do to finish one assignment before turning to the next. Enthusiasm was indeed holding up, but I began to feel that, while offering students a concentrated writing experience which was new and valuable for them, I was doing little to inculcate habits of reviewing, rethinking, and rewriting. My lip service to the ideal of going over, revising and reworking was contradicted, I feared, both by the journalistic models and by the tempo I had set. While I felt satisfaction with the things we were doing, I couldn't avoid a sense of guilt over what we were neglecting. But a fortunate discovery soon lifted this burden and made the point I had missed more tellingly than I could have.

Our school is composed of both boarding and day students. Half the class, therefore, had their papers delivered to their rooms by 7 a.m., while the other half bought theirs at the newsstand on the way to school. The second group usually arrived with a later edition than the first, which usually was an annoyance, since we could not count on uniform location of articles, particularly on the front page, and even found pieces we wanted to talk about missing from some papers. One day, however, we opened to the sports page to discover two different articles by the same hockey writer on the same playoff game. It was an easy task to distinguish the earlier one, an immediate reporting of the game's crucial facts in traditional inverted pyramid form, from the second, a more logically and rhetorically organized essay on the game. They contained the same facts, but the later version had a crisp introduction, a major thesis, interspersed quotations and a concluding observation. We realized that this writer, having done a workmanlike job of conveying his information the first time around, sat down sometime after midnight and carefully reworked his article to make it more readable and penetrating. We might, of course, have come to the same discovery by studying drafts of poems or other artistic productions (see, for example, Charles R. Duke's "How Does the Writer Write?" in *Classroom Practices in Teaching English, 1974-1975: Re-Vision,* pp. 50-53), but the immediacy of seeing rewriting practiced in the hurried world of sports reporting was a very convincing demonstration of its practicality and value for the ordinary writer.

Our final bit of serendipity, if I may call it that, was both more shocking and more meaningful. Just into the fourth week of the course, as I was casting about for a conclusion which would move us off the daily base we had built onto a longer, more complex assignment, I was shocked into understanding just how real our subject matter was. The teaching opportunity I had sought had clearly presented itself.

During a late night robbery in a local shopping center, a Boston patrolman was shot and killed. The newspapers naturally covered the story thoroughly, from front page stories and human background to editorials. I was particularly affected by the incident since my wife was the emergency room nurse who saw the policeman and spoke with his family and fellow officers. The next day I brought into class articles from two different city papers. We discussed at length the murder's treatment in each paper, and how the event produced varied responses over the next few days in letters and articles on the officer's family, gun control and other related topics. I then presented the class with the course's final assignment.

I handed out a description of a similar, but hypothetical, occurrence at a local park in which, under less clear circumstances, a forty-year-old white patrolman and a seventeen-year-old black youth were both killed. (Since the class was quite mixed racially and economically, I wished to give them opportunities for involvement in social issues involving age, class, and color, as well as in law and order questions.) I then suggested some twenty possible assignments based on the sort of newspaper work we had been doing: write a report on the event for the local liberal, conservative or radical paper; conduct an interview with a friend of the officer or the teen-ager; write a letter to the editor as a local black parent, white suburbanite, or city official; editorialize on the killings as an argument for gun control or the death penalty, and so forth. Telling them to write on any four of these topics, I announced that there would be no formal classes for the next six meetings, and that I would be available for consultation during these class hours. They could turn in the papers at their own pace, provided that all four were done by the next-to-last day of the term. I felt this degree of freedom to be necessary if they were to get deeply into the assignment; it was an important opportunity for testing their independence. Yet since this constituted an abrupt change from the mutual and constant reading and writing interaction we had had to that point, I had some fears about the class's abilities to adjust quickly enough.

I need not have worried. Some students came daily with a new paper or revision in hand, while others never appeared until the due date, but every one turned in his or her assignments on time. And each had worked harder on this than on any other assignment all term. One black girl gave me a piece which she had written as a friend of the boy, and told me, with a note of surprise in her voice, that she had cried while writing it; then she submitted a bitter, frustrated, and completely convincing letter as a friend of the policeman. A white boy turned in a letter to the editor from a black mother, so authentic in both voice and perceptions that blacks in the class had to be convinced a white had actually written it. Others did pieces of underground newspaper reportage, polemics by office-seeking city officials, or defensive statements by police spokesmen.

On the final day of the year I simply moved around the class giving each student a chance to read his or her best paper and receive the well-earned admiration of the class. The course's final, and perhaps best, point was made when they all saw how well they and their friends could do when seriously engaged in their work. Several other teachers have since used this last assignment successfully, and I intend to adapt it for future classes, but I know it will never have the immediacy of that first occasion.

"Is There a Box on the Board?" An Exercise in Classification

Judith G. Stitzel

Students wrote more carefully when they learned the effect of language and previous experience on their attempts to classify. Judith G. Stitzel is an associate professor at West Virginia University at Morgantown, West Virginia.

Because composition involves composing, i.e. ordering, we should cultivate in our students a sense of the processes by which their minds work; we should make them aware of their meaning-making power, for unless students can perceive themselves as making choices, they cannot perceive themselves as writing anything other than what they have written or of rewriting something for any other reason than for pleasing us. Although I have not assigned a "theme of classification" for many years, I have become more and more convinced that the process of mind involved is a crucial one, that at the heart of learning is the ability to discover *significant* differences and *significant* similarities and to recognize and acknowledge that in both cases, "significance" depends upon vantage point and is, therefore, relative, and open to discussion.

I asked my English composition class, as a homework assignment, to come up with three bases on which they could classify the contents of the student newspaper, but instead of beginning the period following with a discussion of their assignment, I opened with a communications exercise designed to reveal the effect of language and of previous experience on categorization (classification).

I drew three figures on the board and asked the students to write down all possible ways of describing them. (Figures were taken from Brent D. Ruben and Richard W. Budd, *Human Communications Handbook: Simulations and Games,* [Hayden Book Company, Inc., 1975], pp. 33-34.) For Figure A, the alternatives offered were:

1) three sets of brackets preceded by the right half of a set of brackets,
2) 3 boxes open on top and bottom preceded by half a box,
3) 3 sets of "boxy C's" facing each other preceded by one backward "C," and

Figure A.

Figure B.

Figure C.

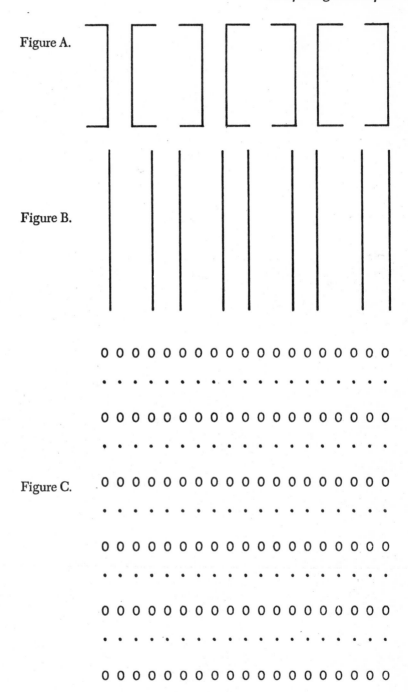

4) 3 "I's" with fat centers followed by a backwards "L" with a line on top.

For Figure B, the alternatives offered were:

1) nine lines organized 1, 2, 2, 2, 2,
2) four sets of parallel single lines preceded by a single vertical line,
3) one single line and four tubes,
4) one single line and four columns, and
5) three lanes of an expressway.

For Figure C, everyone suggested 11 alternating horizontal rows of 22 circles or dots, beginning and ending with dots.

After eliciting all of the responses — it took a little coaxing to get some of them out; several students couldn't quite believe that I wanted theirs, even though it was only "slightly" different from someone else's — I asked the students to generalize about what they had just done, to isolate some of the characteristics of classification. They were confused, and I realized that I had begun on too high a level of generality and/or that I was assuming their self-consciousness about just the process that I was hoping to make them self-conscious of. I did two things. I rephrased my requests ("Would you talk about what you have just done?" "Why did you describe the figures the way that you did?"), and when that still didn't seem to elicit a response I followed up by rephrasing specific questions to specific people.

"Why did you say brackets?"

"Because I'm familiar with them from math and chemistry."

"Oh, you mean concentration brackets? I didn't think of those."

"I didn't think of them either; I thought of the brackets on a typewriter."

I pointed out that in both cases, past experience was affecting, if not determining, the choices made.

"Why did you say 'box'?"

"Because that's what was on the board."

"But not everybody said 'box.' Why did you?"

No answer.

"Is there in fact a box on the board?"

Still no answer.

"What's on the board?"

"Chalk marks," somebody finally ventured, facetiously, I think, but I grabbed at it.

"Right. Chalk marks on a board. That's probably demonstrable. But where's the box?"

"The eye and mind want to make sense of what they see."

"The imagination sees the box."

"Well, if the box is just chalk on the board, so are the words." (I had written out several key words as they had been offered earlier, e.g. 'brackets,' 'box,' etc.)

Another good-natured (?) taunt and again, not proud, I grabbed.

"That's true. The letters and words on the board are chalk. They do not carry their meaning in themselves; we bring meaning to them. 'Our eyes and mind want to make sense of what they see,'" I quoted the student back to the class.

I then put three Hebrew letters on the board and asked the students to describe what they saw. (French or German or any other language could have been used, but using another alphabetical system did make the point more dramatically; not only didn't the students understand the meaning of the words, but only one student even recognized the letters as "letters.")

"Just scrawls."

"Nonsense."

"A design."

It was a fine opportunity to demonstrate that meaning, like beauty, is in the eye and mind of the beholder.

"What is the least you'd have to know before you could have used the word 'tube' in your description of B?"

"You'd have to see it as something thin."

"Okay, but what if you did see it as something thin, what if you felt that 'column' was too fat, what would still be necessary before you could use 'tube'?"

Some tooth-pulling here, and then,

You'd have to know the word 'tube.'"

Sometimes the facts that seem too ludicrously obvious to mention are actually hard to recognize, and it is for that reason doubly important that we bring them to the surface. What we are least conscious of we have least control over.

"Okay. Our language, the words we know — how many and which ones — limits or expands our ability to think, to conceptualize. How else did either language or past experience affect your choices?"

"Past experience caused us all to talk about horizontal lines in Figure C. Orientals might have talked about vertical lines."

"Is that 'past experience' in the same sense that recognizing brackets from chemistry is?"

"No, in a broader sense."

"Do you have another word for it?"

"How about 'environment'?"

"How about 'culture'?"

Interestingly enough, this discussion itself provided an example of the way in which language, i.e. having the word "culture" as part of one's active vocabulary, affects the related processes of classification and discrimination, of finding similarities and finding differences.

"What about where we're sitting? That might have something to do with what we see. What looks like a box from one angle may not look like one from another."

I hadn't thought of that one, and I was very pleased that the student had, since it allowed me to move easily from his concrete example of the importance of point of view to a more abstract consideration of perspective as a major variable in classification. With this in mind, I moved into the homework assignment.

The first thing I discovered when asking for sample answers was that the students had misunderstood the assignment and/or that I had not been sufficiently clear in making it. Not one student had come up with three bases of classification; in fact, no one came up with any. What they had instead were the categories themselves, chosen on a number of bases: news, ads, students' news, photos, art, cartoons, etc. To get them to realize that the category any individual item fits in depends upon the basis of classification, I asked them if Oliphant and Doonesbury, nationally syndicated cartoons, were necessarily in the same category as Pinball Morgan, a local creation. I was hoping to stimulate the awareness that though all three were cartoons, they would not be in the same category if we divided along lines of student-produced and syndicated materials. But thanks to the constant overturn of even the best laid inductive methods, I got something else, at least as useful — scornful laughter, followed by "Pinball Morgan is in a class by itself."

"*What do you mean?*"

"It just is."

"*Why? How is it different?*"

"You just can't talk about them together. Oliphant is in a different class from Pinball, that's all!"

The note of frustration frequently signals a process that is below the level of awareness, the students experiencing their judgments as if they came involuntarily and necessarily, as if the students did not really have a choice, make a decision. As far as I could see, the students were using "class" in these interchanges without any awareness that they were classifying, and I took the opportunity to point out that classification, far from being a figment of Hans Guth's or my collective unconscious, was an actual mental process, used and useful, in sorting out the universe. I also took the opportunity to get further into the basis of their distinction.

"Why are they in different classes?"
"One is good, one is bad."
"Okay, but in what way good, in what way bad?"
"One seems political and the other is just plain stupid."
"Does that mean that something political can never be stupid?"
Post-Watergate cynical chuckles.
"One seems informed, the other uninformed."

We were still on slippery ground, of course, classifying according to a subjective (what constitutes well-informed?) rather than an objective (what is syndicated?) criterion, but we were, I thought, above ground in a way we hadn't been before.

The most important part of the exercise — connecting the assignment with the earlier discussion — came the next period. I undertook to reveal the similarity between the processes the students had used to "see" the figures and to "divide" the newspaper into categories. I tried to demonstrate that in both processes, they saw something as part of a whole, which could as reasonably have been seen as part of some other whole, whether it was a matter of seeing a "]" in Figure A as the left hand side of a "fat I" rather than as a "single backward boxy C" or of seeing Pinball Morgan as a member of the class "cartoons" rather than of the class "locally-produced materials." And I tried to demonstrate that while we are, in fact, limited in our perceptions by past experiences and language, we also have considerable control in choosing which perceptions to use, on which occasions, and for which purposes. The girl who originally saw Figure A as having a "backward L with a line on top" admitted that if she were describing the figure to someone else, she would probably substitute "a backward square C" as less ambiguous. Others recognized that dividing the newspaper into student-produced and syndicated materials might be valuable if they wanted to support the position that the newspaper should be kept as a training ground for journalism students, while categories arrived at through other divisions, e.g. news versus advertisements or items of interest to the university community, local community, and general public, might yield information useful for different purposes.

By no means do I wish to suggest that one or two class periods spent on an exercise of this kind will magically guarantee students a new sense of their meaning-making potential. Quite the contrary, I would argue that unless this awareness is reinforced by the overall structure of the composition class and a reasonable proportion of the students' other educational experiences, it will probably not affect them at all. But I feel certain that unless students are aware of themselves as active participants in the learning process, they cannot take full delight in or responsibility for what they know or for what they write. I don't think it is at all accidental that the same girl who called the figure on the board a "box" because "that's what it was" had, the previous week, during a discussion of the difficulties associated with defining, told the class somewhat worriedly that she wasn't having any difficulties. She knew what "good taste" was because her design book had told her in chapter one. The thought that she might have another definition, and that *her* definition might serve her own purposes, apparently had not occurred to her. Unaware of the mind's active role in making sense of the world, she'd become accustomed to looking outside herself both for direction and for meaning. We owe it to ourselves and our students to help them look inside. It is not enough to give our students knowledge; we must insure that they gain confidence in themselves as knowers as well.

Students Write Their Own Bicentennial Ballads

Mariana Gibson
Bessemer City Schools
Bessemer, Alabama

Capitalizing on the simplicity of the ballad form and upon the fact that much that happened in the fateful years of 1775, 1776, and 1777 was recorded and preserved in song, the teacher conducting a discussion of the revolutionary era can inspire some twentieth-century ballads about eighteenth-century events and treat the class to an experience in creativity.

Using the most familiar rhymes, like Yankee Doodle, which has its own revolutionary implications, teacher and class can read through the lines and beat out the rhythm:

O Yankee Doodle went to town
A riding on his pony;
He stuck a feather in his cap
And called it macaroni!
And there was Captain Washington
Upon a slapping stallion
And all the men and boys around,
I guess there was a million!

Since the rhythm is simple and easily scanned, the discussion can be channeled into the origin of the term "yankee," the meaning of the term "macaroni," and the significance of Captain Washington. Here the teacher may shift the emphasis to explore familiar ballad topics and present-day songs that might fit the traditional ballad form. Examples might be "Ode to Billy Joe" or "The Night They Drove Dixie Down." Some stanzas could be projected onto a screen or written on a chalk board so the class could scan the verses.

At this point the class is ready to write their own ballads, using topics from our revolutionary era. Suggestions from the class can be listed: the Continental Congress, the ride of Paul Revere and William Dawes, the stand at Concord bridge, the tax on tea. The more familiar the theme is, the easier it will be for students to catch the creative mood. If they can join in as the ballad takes form on the chalkboard or the overhead screen, they can enjoy the feeling for the rhythm and the fun of a group effort.

After creating one four-line verse — be it good or otherwise — other possible first lines for verses of the same topic or for ballads describing other events of the revolutionary era might be suggested by the class and listed on the board or the screen. Depending on whether the ballads are to be a class effort or individual products, the teacher pursues the discussion in class or allows the students to try writing ballads of their own for credit.

Interesting or outstanding verses produced by this activity should be noted by the school by being published in the school paper or in a bicentennial publication. At the least they should be typed or printed attractively and displayed on a classroom or topical bulletin board.

Writing to Clarify Values

Stopping the March through Georgia

Deanna M. Gutschow

*A conference approach to teaching writing can help
the students find a voice. Deanna M. Gutschow
teaches at Whitefish Bay High School,
Whitefish Bay, Wisconsin, and is president of
Wisconsin Council of Teachers of English.*

I have long believed that personal experience writing can involve a person in a process of self-definition and self-discovery. Yet many of the papers I received from the juniors and seniors in my composition classes were either totally lacking in insight or illumined by fitful flashes.

Then I began to stress revision and to hold individual conferences with students after they had written one complete version of a paper. Once I began intensive conferencing, I found that students' papers were often a dull recital of facts, not because they lacked insight, or the ability to exercise an informing perspective, but because they had either stopped writing before they had fully discovered what they wanted to say, or had failed to express the significance of a certain experience, even though they knew what it had meant to them.

By asking students questions about their papers, I've come to see that the first draft of a student's personal narrative is more often the product of "thinking-as-remembering" than of "thinking-as-discovery." And the "finished" essay turned in to the teacher is, more often than not, just a neatly copied version of that first draft.

In "thinking-as-remembering," students call to mind images and feelings about a particular experience. What they remember initially is often confusing, vague and contradictory, and this lack of clarity comes out in the first draft. It is also likely to contain "verbal shorthand," which means more to the writer than to the reader. Another problem is that the pattern of emphasis in the first version of a paper is often inadequate, largely because a student begins the paper at a point too early in the experience, or uses too much detail, often irrelevant, in the initial process of verbalizing it. Then, by the time the student reaches the most significant part, he or she has begun to run out of energy (and time), and the detail grows thinner and thinner. The paper becomes expository summary, just when the writer should be involving the reader most fully through the use of sensory detail

96

or detailed exposition. The pattern of emphasis in the first version, in other words, is shaped more often by a student's declining energy and deadline, than by a critical sense.

"Thinking-as-discovery," on the other hand, occurs when the writer begins to look at what he or she has written in a detached, critical manner, and to reflect both on what is written and how it is written. Through "thinking-as-discovery," the writer articulates a personal perspective and thus is able to shape the material, to select the kind of relevant detail that best reveals his or her attitude toward the events described.

"Thinking-as-discovery" does occur, of course, when the student is trying to remember an experience, not just after it is written down once, but the novice is usually far less skillful than the trained writer at exercising both types of thinking simultaneously.

Janet Emig, in her study of the composing process of eight high school seniors has noted that one major difference between student writers and experienced writers is that the former are engaged in a linear, lock-step process when they write (what Dr. Emig calls the "Marchin' through Georgia" method). The student writer typically does little prefiguring and moves inexorably from the beginning of the composition to the end, with no major reformulation or revising. For the experienced writer, however, the act of writing is characterized by "recursiveness" — planning, writing, rethinking, and rewriting occur and reoccur throughout that process instead of in a linear sequence.[1]

A second major difference between typical eleventh or twelfth graders and skilled writers is that the former rarely know how to take a critical stance regarding their writing unless they are shown, whereas the latter know how to "talk" to themselves *as they write.*

Many professional writers have commented that when they are writing, two "voices" seem to engage in a dialogue inside their heads — one voice "dictates" the material to be put down on paper, while the other views the written material critically, raising questions about its logic, precision or accuracy, and about how meaningful it will be to a reader. I think this technique can be taught to any student of average ability. Through my conferences with students, I try to show how a dialogue can be carried on about what they have written. This intensive give-and-take conference involves the student in a process that he or she can internalize and therefore use when writing or revising alone. This method, of course, takes much more time than the traditional method of conferencing in which the student

---

[1] Janet Emig, *The Composing Processes of Twelfth Graders* (Urbana, Illinois: National Council of Teachers of English, 1971).

is a passive recipient of the teacher's words of wisdom. However, the conferences tend to grow shorter toward the end of the semester as students develop their ability to use this technique.

I also try to engage students in the "thinking-as-discovery" process through class discussions that focus on two papers describing similar experiences. One remains just an interesting story, while the other uses an experience as a metaphor for some personal concern (perhaps universally shared, i.e. self-image, controlling one's life, etc.). For example, we compare one paper in which a student describes the thrill of hunting deer but fails to invest that hunt with any real significance, and another in which the student perceives the deer hunt as "rites of passage," as an initiation into the adult male world of his father and uncle.

In conferencing on a personal experience paper, I guard against forcing students to invest an experience with meaning when it has little for them, or insisting that they reveal their personal concerns even when they are not willing to. In those few instances where a student is definitely opposed to writing about significant experiences, I encourage writing about whatever topic he or she feels comfortable with. But I have found that students are not so much opposed to expressing genuine concerns as they are perplexed about how to pinpoint them in connection with specific experiences and how to express them intelligibly to a reader.

For example, one of my students this semester, in response to the first major assignment, wrote five typewritten pages on a "challenging experience" — a week-long bike trip he had taken with a friend. For the first four pages Rick described the uneventful two-day ride from Whitefish Bay to a state park in northern Wisconsin, including irrelevant details about the bike rack that held his camping equipment, the clothes he and his companion wore, the scenery, and what they ate for breakfast the first morning at the state park. On page five, Rick finally stated, "the ultimate challenge was still ahead of us" and went on to describe an approaching storm whose high winds made the return trip difficult and which dumped four inches of rain on their tent when they camped that night. He also stated that during the final leg of their trip, they not only had to ride over twenty miles after dark, but they had to contend with strong winds.

In his concluding paragraph Rick wrote, "At the beginning of the trip, it felt good to get away from my parents, society, etc., but it also felt good to get back. Not because I missed people or things, but because we proved that two teenagers could do something if they set their minds to it."

Rick had stated the trip's significance in that paragraph, but nothing in the preceding paragraphs suggested that his attitude toward the trip was influenced by his parents' belief that he wouldn't be able to complete it.

Here is an edited transcript of two sections of my taped conference with Rick which illustrates how my questioning was intended to engage him in "thinking-as-discovery" and to provide him with a model dialectic method.

Me: After reading your paper, I wondered why you took so long to get to what you call "the ultimate challenge." It seems to me that by the time you get to the "ultimate challenge," you've put in so much time on minor detail, you've run out of steam, and there's nothing there. The challenge is given less space than describing the things you put on your bike rack at the beginning of the paper. Isn't your paper ending just when it really should have begun?

Rick: Uh . . . see, really the challenge is not the trip itself. It was the fact of doing it. Sure, the trip was challenging, but the actual challenge was . . . I was proving a point, not so much doing it for the fun of it.

Me: (Being deliberately dense) But the proving of the point meant being able to complete the trip, right? It meant being able to withstand the most unpleasant, not the most pleasant aspects of the trip. . . . If your trip had been as pleasant at the end as it was at the beginning, it wouldn't have posed much of a challenge. Yes, there was a challenge in the distance you covered. But when you were faced with dangerous weather, you could have hopped a bus, or called home and said, 'Dad, come and pick us up,' right? When you say, 'we proved two teenagers could do something,' did your parents think you would not be able to do it, or what?

Rick: They didn't think it was within my ability . . . that being brought up with rides to school — junk like that . . .

Me: Did they say that specifically to you?

Rick: They didn't say it exactly like that. But they said, "If you ever run into trouble, just give us a call and we'll come pick you up."

Me: And you felt this meant they thought you would act the same way you had previously?

Rick: (His tone becomes sharper) They didn't have faith in me . . . It was like they were waiting at the phone, waiting for it to ring, so they could go and pick me up.

Me: You thought they were, or they actually were waiting at the phone?

Rick: That's what I *thought* they were doing. And Chris, his mother . . . one time his mother said (when we were on the way back) that she would come and pick us up . . . so we just hung up the phone and left so she wouldn't.

Me: I think you've brought something to this paper now that was there all along, but which you didn't bring out very clearly. (I switch to questions about tightening the paper, and Rick sees that he could begin his revision with the return trip just before the weather became stormy.) Now the question is, how could you make the reader aware of the attitude of your parents, of Chris' parents, and that you were trying to prove something to them?

Rick: Do you think a flashback . . . to get to a certain part, and then to show my parents saying, "They'll never make it"?

Me: What do you think? Can you see how that might be worked in?

Rick: Well, if I start at the point where things went from bad to worse . . . and then calling home . . . yeah, that would be all right.
(As I continue to raise questions about the difficulties of the trip home, Rick mentions a problem he had not alluded to in his first version — keeping up with Chris who had a lighter bike and more physical stamina.)

Me: So not only was there the challenge of the bad biking conditions, but you were traveling with someone who was physically stronger, so you had to worry about keeping up with him, too. Were you at all concerned about what Chris might think of you if you fell behind or wanted to stop?

Rick: Yeah, I was riding very fast, at least for my ability. I think it's 31 miles from Port Washington . . . and we were zipping along at 20 miles an hour.

Me: When you came home, what did your parents say?

Rick: The usual . . . how was your trip?

Me: Did you play down the problems?

Rick: It you tell your parents too many of the problems, you don't get to go again. We didn't tell them we headed north on a major highway with a lot of truck traffic . . . that would have been the end of it . . . and we didn't tell them about the dog that attacked me, and the trouble with the wind — until later.

Me: Why don't you end on that note — what you didn't feel you could tell your parents, because you were proud of what you had accomplished, and you were afraid they wouldn't let you go again. . . .

When students do begin to engage in an inner dialectic with themselves about their writing, some of them complain that it feels unnatural. As one student told me after beginning her second major assignment, "Once I started my paper, I found myself 'writing for my conference,' and trying to interpret what your questions and objections would be. This bothered me, because I felt it inhibited my writing."

When I asked her if this meant she felt she was writing to please me, rather than to achieve greater clarity, she replied, "I'm writing to please myself, but I'm questioning what I write much more now than I ever did before. That's really slowing me down, making me think a lot harder about what I'm trying to say."

To me, this is the inhibition that usually precedes acquiring a complex technique. Rather than enslaving the student, it can only lead to the true freedom of the writer who looks inward rather than outward for critical evaluation.

Personal Growth and the Teaching of Writing

Margaret Labby

Teaching in a workshop-type program that scheduled formal writing after a free writing experience, Margaret Labby emphasized student evaluation at Lincoln High School, Portland, Oregon.

Our writing elective has expanded from two classes five years ago to eight for upperclassmen and eight for underclassmen this year and has become the most popular elective offered by the school. Having taught in the program since it began, I am convinced that a writing class provides a superb opportunity to encourage personal growth as well as the development of writing skills.

I have worked out a method that accomplishes both objectives with reasonable success. I try to provide a relaxed and noncompetitive atmosphere where students spend most of their class time either writing papers, listening to what others have written, or working together cooperatively in small groups helping to improve each other's writing. There are only two kinds of writing assignments: free writing and formal compositions.

At least twice a week students are involved in free writing — writing for fifteen minutes or longer without worrying about technical skills or organization. This is a new and liberating experience for most and an excellent shock tactic for overcoming the "I can't write" syndrome suffered alike by remedial and honor roll students. At first they may write about anything. Later more focused assignments provide variety. They are asked to respond to a piece of music, a cartoon or a picture; to write their own endings to stories I read them; to describe the sounds heard outside the room, inside the room and inside themselves (an exercise I picked up while visiting a school in England); to compose a short story incorporating two completely unrelated sentences, one they write and keep and one they pull out of a hat; to describe the guided fantasies I occasionally take them on; to write a dialogue showing how a vice-principal would handle a student discovered to have marijuana in her purse (other role-playing situations are equally effective). The final mid-term and end-of-term free writing is a self-evaluation that forces students to examine their own progress and provides me with an excellent source of feedback.

Students enjoy both the unfocused and focused assignments. They enjoy the variety of the assignments, the occasional opportunity to let their mind wander, the freedom to write with only the one requirement of filling 1½ pages, and the chance to hear what others have written. I am as amazed as the students at the variety and originality of the responses. Comments from student self-evaluations are insightful: "Free writing has helped me see parts of myself on paper." "It helps my writing ability, but even more, helps me think out problems I have to learn to cope with." "Free writing gives me a chance to relax and speak what's on my mind." "After a student has done . . . free writing, he finds it easier to pull ideas out of his head and express them on paper."

Designed to increase fluency and encourage creativity, free writing has the added benefit of providing a fun-and-games atmosphere to the classroom, a pleasant contrast to the more disciplined writing required in their weekly 1½ to 2 page formal compositions. Although free to select their own topics and genre, students must revise, reshape and rewrite these papers according to traditional composition standards. No paper is considered complete unless one or more rough drafts is stapled underneath the carefully rewritten final copy.

The rigorous discipline required for formal papers is made palatable by having students work together in small groups on two separate occasions. After having prepared a first draft at home, students read it aloud to the group for feedback, a process that allows them to hear how it sounds and feel how it is received by their peers. Often they come to the group for help with a specific problem, such as how to introduce a topic or end a story more effectively or how to make a paper sound better. Many students revise their papers considerably after these sessions. One or two days elapse for such revision at home. Then the group meets a second time to edit the final copy, correcting any spelling, punctuation,or grammatical errors before finally submitting the papers to me.

I spend a number of periods with the class at the beginning of the semester exploring the advantage of "positive reinforcement" over the "putdown" as well as the need for being supportive and nonjudgmental when suggesting changes or improvements. We discuss papers written by students I have had in the past to learn what to look for and to practice how to make constructive comments. A more difficult problem is how to divide the class into groups. Depending on the make-up of the class, I allow students to select their own groups or I select the groups myself. Whether the groups stay together for only a term or an entire semester depends on the effectiveness with which they function.

Most students find the group process rewarding although there are always a few who refuse to participate. Those who do participate find their papers are improved, and their repertoire of both subject matter and genre expanded. Listening to a story written by a member of the group encourages others to try their hand at fiction; students occasionally discover untapped creative and imaginative capacities. Furthermore, the small groups provide students with a welcome opportunity to develop skills in interpersonal relationships. Everyone, the academic and nonacademic (the writing classes attract students of all abilities), the shy and the outgoing, has something to contribute. Comments from their self-evaluations are again enlightening: "The group has taught me how to accept other people's criticism and helpful suggestions without any bitterness or resentment." "Working on rough drafts... has taught me how to improve another's work without making him feel like a failure. It has taught me more about getting along with people." "Group work helps me learn to be honest with other people and to listen with an open mind."

The group process has the added advantage of reducing the time it takes me to read and write comments on these papers. My time is further reduced by our competent lay reader who marks technical errors (no one will be surprised that the groups fail to catch them all) and coordinates her corrections with class exercises, concentrating in turn on spelling, punctuation, grammar and usage. An essential part of the writing program, she relieves me of the negative role of identifying errors and allows me to maintain a positive and supportive role. Rather than making students defensive by telling them what is wrong with the content, organization, or style of their papers, I ask questions designed to help them identify their own flaws or weaknesses. I write a generous critique and give a grade rewarding effort and improvement to all students who have turned in papers on time and worked hard revising rough drafts. Those showing only minimal interest in the class and little effort at revision merely receive a grade.

The method described above reflects my attempt to provide a healthy balance between cognitive and affective learning — to give students an opportunity to develop skills of critical thinking and to learn a variety of writing techniques in an atmosphere that also fosters personal growth and development. There are, of course, many problems. Not all students enjoy the relaxed atmosphere or the lack of pressure. Some students think unfocused free writing is a "waste of time." Some prefer not to participate in the group process.

By far the majority enjoy and profit from this method. By the end of the semester even the weakest is able to focus on a single idea and develop it with details and examples. Many have learned how to write a piece of fiction with a reasonable degree of unity and coherence. Most have improved their technical competency to some degree, and all have learned the benefit of having an outsider edit their work as professional writers do. Best of all, many have discovered that writing can be a useful tool to release or explore feelings, and a surprising number have found that although writing is difficult, even drudgery, it can also bring pleasure and satisfaction.

Values Clarification, Journals, and the Freshman Writing Course

Robert A. Rennert

Teachers in the author's freshman writing course combined two popular classroom practices. Robert A. Rennert teaches at Findlay College, Findlay, Ohio.

"I liked writing in the journal because it helped me to see myself when I reread the journal entries."

"This journal has helped me to get my thoughts down on paper. It has made me realize how much I have learned and how much more there is to learn."

"Through my entries in this journal, I have been able to determine my values, see what I am, and find out what I want to be. The journals were valuable in that they brought out my bad points as well as my good points."

These student comments are typical of those made at the end of a term of Findlay College's required writing course, "Self Awareness through Writing." No doubt the novelty of keeping a journal prompted some students' positive response. But the primary cause of general student satisfaction was a carefully planned series of values clarification exercises which formed the core of the majority of the journal entries.

Values clarification techniques and journal-keeping may seem unrelated, yet they work well together. Both activities assume that the process of discovery has more realistic educational merit than traditional attempts to impose "content" (a given set of values or a theory of writing). The values clarification theorists' insistence on the need for a person to manifest the values he or she has chosen finds a natural outlet in the written affirmation of a journal entry. The possibility of values being rethought and modified by new awareness is matched by the contingent nature of journal material, its susceptibility to being shaped and reshaped again and again.

Realizing the compatability of the procedures, I experimented with the combination in my freshman writing course. I had asked students to keep journals in previous writing courses, but I had never been completely satisfied with them. Often students seemed bothered by inertia ("What do

I write about?"); students who did write were often frustrated because they felt their entries were trivial, dealing repeatedly with inconsequential matters like the previous night's water fight in the dorm. By using values clarification materials as part of regular journal exercises, I overcame these problems. Confronted with significant questions and problems, students moved off dead center and were stimulated to discover, through writing, knowledge about their values and attitudes.

My primary resource for the exercises was *Values Clarification: A Handbook of Practical Strategies for Teachers and Students* (New York: Hart, 1972). The book, a compendium of 79 "strategies," can be used in many ways to engage students in reflection about their values. It is impossible to detail all these ways here, but the following methods suggest a range of possibilities.

Frequently I employed one of the strategies as the core of a three-part daily exercise. The first few minutes of class were spent in free writing, a warm-up period to get the students into the mood for writing. Then I presented a strategy — a values problem to be worked out, a consideration of possible alternatives to a given situation, or a question about a daily activity which might reveal values — in order to direct their attention to a specific, significant values issue. I concluded the exercise by asking them to free associate, in writing, with an object or situation related as closely as possible to the strategy. In short, the journal entry became a way to help students get at matters of personal concern, a method implementing the assumption that good writing is often the product of personal conviction, the intimate involvement of writer with subject matter.

The handbook conveniently groups those strategies which work well in series. I found it helpful to order them according to two purposes: one, to make the students aware of their value systems at the beginning of the term, and another, to help them find material for different kinds of writing. I began the term with a value survey in which students were asked to rank-order items on two lists, one a list of values such as equality and pleasure and the other a list of human qualities like ambition and forgiveness. After the ranking I asked them to explain in writing what influenced their choices. I also asked them to list their choices (anonymously) on a separate form which I collected. By collating their rankings, I got a feeling for the general value scheme of the class as a whole and thus gained a greater awareness of my students' attitudes. (If a teacher has several sections of the same writing course, such information could be valuable and help one adapt to the needs of each class.)

By choosing appropriate strategies as the term progressed, I engaged students in different rhetorical tasks ranging from personal narratives to comparison/contrast essays. For example, about midway through the term, when I thought it was desirable that they affirm some of the values they had been discovering, I asked them to write argumentative essays on subjects of personal concern. To help them get at those concerns, I presented them with "forced choice" and "spread of opinion" strategies which made them confront controversial issues about which they had strong opinions. I then instructed them to review their responses, to investigate values and attitudes which were opposite to their own, and to formulate well-reasoned position papers.

The strategies are adaptable not only for varying kinds of writing assignments but also for exercises which emphasize the process of writing. "Pattern search" strategies, for example, can be segmented quite easily into daily writings forming a cumulative series. An initial exercise might call for a wealth of specific details (e.g. about the kind, color, use and qualities of items in one's wardrobe). Succeeding exercises require the student to order that list of details according to some principle (e.g. what I want my clothes to say about me) and, finally, to formulate a paragraph or an essay stating and supporting a conclusion.

Near the end of the term, I used strategies which asked students to think about values they wanted to develop in the future. For instance, they were requested to write their own obituaries containing the things for which they wanted to be remembered by friends and relatives. They also wrote self-contracts, written promises to themselves to develop some attitude or skill or to change in some way. As their final assignment, they wrote an autobiographical statement which demonstrated that they had reviewed their journal entries and reached some conclusions about what they had learned about themselves. In this way the course content, their own writing, became a meaningful learning experience.

Exploring Writing Systems

Composition Skills and Career Education

Robert C. Small

Written composition skills develop when given more than a surface application to career education activities. Robert C. Small, Jr., is associate professor at Virginia Polytechnical Institute and State University, Blacksburg, Virginia.

More and more schools are being asked to revise their programs to include greater emphasis on career education. The pressure is coming from all sides: businessmen who feel that schools do not prepare students well to seek employment, parents who worry that their children will leave school to join the unemployment lines, students who see little relation between much that they have to do in school and the practical necessity of earning a living. Many professional educators, frequently but not exclusively from the vocational education areas, are also energetically advising a shift to career education throughout the school.

English teachers, perhaps more than most high school teachers, have difficulty responding to this call for career education since many feel that what they do in their classes relates more to the noncareer aspects of their students' future lives. The area of written composition skills, however, is in many ways closely related to career education. The English teacher performs a major career education service by creating students who can write clearly, who can, when they want to, conform to the traditional rules of spelling and mechanics, and perhaps most important, who are able to deal effectively with the requirements of different types of writing. On the other hand, many of the specific career-oriented writing skills which English teachers are asked to teach do not fit easily into the types of writing with which they have been prepared to deal. Consequently, teachers have often presented the skills involved in writing letters of application and in filling out application forms in isolation from the rest of the program. Aside from some emphasis on mechanical accuracy, such lessons have generally had little connection to the rest of the program and have, in fact, seemed to many English teachers more appropriately a part of some other subject such as distributive education.

English teachers, usually at the request of the guidance department (and rather unwillingly), have occasionally assigned their students a report on some topic such as "My Future Occupation" and tried to use the assignment as a means of teaching research skills. Lifted in large part from career pamphlets and encyclopedias, such reports have usually been less than successful, either from the career or from the English point of view. In addition to being tedious and irrelevant, such reports have failed because no effort was made to help the student to understand and to feel what being in his or her career choice is like and to articulate that feeling. Instead, external, largely factual information was all that the student was asked for or given. It is possible, however, to plan a unit which will provide each student with many opportunities to learn about and practice a variety of writing skills while at the same time exploring a career from both the outside (applicant) and the inside (practitioner).

Phase One: Outside

In such a unit, the students would begin in the traditional manner by examining factual information about a selected career and summarizing those facts in a brief presentation using the skills of outlining and summarizing. Not a research report, there would be no pretense that the result was anything but a condensation of one or more sources. From this summary, the students would then write a list of the characteristics that they have which suit them for that career. At the same time, they would examine want ads or similar materials appropriate to this career and obtain the names and addresses of businesses, agencies, institutions, etc. which employ people from that occupation. They would choose one and write a letter requesting information about work possibilities. They would also ask for copies of job applications, descriptions of application procedures, etc. When such materials have been obtained, the students would go through the formal application procedures for employment used in the career, including possibly a simulated submission to whatever certification processes or examinations may be used in the field.

Phase Two: Inside

Up to this point, the unit would resemble many efforts by English teachers to create simulated situations for the writing of job applications, and it is at this point that most units conclude. Unfortunately, however, such a unit concentrates only on the externals of the career under consideration, and the writing exercises and skills are of a rather low level. If, however, the unit were to continue by asking the students to pretend that they had, in fact, entered the career under consideration, many additional writing skills could be included. By reading biographies and autobiographies, novels, short stories, and essays by and about members of a particular career, students would attempt to develop a sense of what it is like to be a person in that career. They might also examine appropriate specialized materials such as journals, manuals, and books.

This second phase would require various types of writing. Students would be expected to interview a member of the chosen career and present a written report in the manner of journalistic interviews with well-known people. They would also write a narrative in which they attempted to present the details of the public life of a person in that career. They might also write several short papers from this person's point of view, such as a letter to the editor of a local newspaper reacting to some issue or event, a letter to a colleague, or a report to a superior. The particular skills involved in each type of composition would, of course, be studied as a preliminary to the writing. Descriptive writing would focus on the details of the place of work and would probably require a visit to such a place. Impressionistic writing would involve efforts to capture the various moods of the career and those who pursue it, and character sketches could be written about fellow workers, clients, etc. Again, the particular skills involved in each type of writing would be examined as a part of the writing situation.

Finally, in the role of an established practitioner of the career, students would be asked to prepare a job description to be given to someone considering entering that field. They would also prepare an advertisement for a job opening, using the form appropriate to the career, and develop application materials and procedures. The final step in the unit would consist of reviewing their own applications from Phase One, deciding whether or not to hire themselves on that basis, preparing a report to some appropriate authority explaining the decision, and writing a letter to the applicant informing him or her of the decision.

Thus, in such a unit, each student would practice the general skills of composing and also the particular skills involved in the following types of writing:

1. a summary,
2. a list of character elements,
3. a letter asking for information,
4. a job application,
5. a journalistic interview,

6. a narrative,
7. a letter to a newspaper editor,
8. a friendly letter,
9. a report to a superior,
10. a description,
11. an impressionistic piece capturing a mood,
12. several character sketches,
13. a job description,
14. an advertisement,
15. an application form, and
16. a letter to a job applicant.

This composition unit moves students from the outside of a proposed career to the inside, guiding them from an uninformed novice to the expert who makes decisions about job applicants. Because of the emphasis on the inside details of the career, the unit would provide the student with a simulated situation for the practice of many different composing skills, all of which, even the more "creative," would have a meaningful and practical application. Such a unit, then, would meet the challenge of career education and, at the same time, allow for activities appropriate to the objectives of the English composition program.

The Case Folder Approach to the Research Paper

Edward Deluzain

*A system for making their own casebooks improved
the quality of research papers in the
senior high school classes of Edward Deluzain,
on the superintendent's staff of the Bay County
School System, Panama City, Florida.*

Every year in English classes across the United States, teachers and students together endure the drudgery, and sometimes the pain, of producing The Research Paper. Much of the drudgery, and some of the pain, comes not so much from the actual writing of the paper as from the accompanying activities of locating references in the library and of sorting through what sometimes becomes huge amounts of information. However, the process of writing the research paper can be greatly simplified for both student and teacher if the teacher adopts the concept of the "casebook" that has long been popular in freshman English courses in college.

One of the serious drawbacks to the use of commercially published casebooks in high school English programs is that they are often too expensive for strained departmental budgets; another equally serious drawback is that there may not be casebooks available on all of the current topics of interest. However, neither drawback is sufficient to prevent an English teacher from adopting the casebook concept in teaching the research paper. When casebooks are in short supply, develop your own — or have your students develop them.

The homemade casebook to which I refer is not a book at all, but rather a folder. The case folder consists of the same kinds of things that a casebook consists of, and it can be kept on file in the classroom or departmental office. Case folders can be developed and collected over a period of several years with the result that students have available to them hundreds of miniature libraries to use in writing research papers. Since the purpose of having students use case folders is to give them an opportunity to write a paper within a limited framework, there is no particularly compelling reason why the folders have to be updated as new material is printed. Furthermore, the case folders can be made more flexible than a casebook by the inclusion of speeches recorded on audio cassettes and outstanding papers written by students who use the folders. The inclusion of the papers has the

114

added advantages of providing students with models written by their peers and of preventing good papers from being handed in by students who are not the authors of the papers.

It is obvious that case folders do not come into existence by themselves, but it is possible, and probably very desirable, to have students develop case folders as part of a unit on reference skills. English teachers are generally expected to assume the responsibility of teaching students how to use the library card catalog, the *Readers' Guide to Periodical Literature,* and other reference aids, and the process of learning how to use the various research resources available to the student can be made more meaningful if it results in a useful product such as a case folder. The steps in the development of case folders may be as follows:

First, students are given instruction in the use of whatever references, catalogs, guides, indexes, bibliographies, abstracts, etc., are available.

Second, students should be asked to select a subject that they are interested in and to practice their reference skills by locating information on their chosen subject. The teacher should devise some kind of system to insure that several students do not choose the same, or very closely related, subjects, since duplication is likely to tax limited resources.

Third, the teacher or librarian should make available to students as many unwanted back issues of magazines, newspapers, and journals as possible. A good case folder should contain entries that have been clipped from periodicals and supplied with full bibliographical data, so it will be necessary for students to cut out certain articles. Friends and colleagues will probably be willing to donate old periodicals that can be mutilated for this purpose, and some newsstands are willing to let schools have back issues of magazines that they have been unable to sell. In some cities post office officials are willing to make available to schools the magazines and newspapers that they are unable to deliver, so resources should not be difficult to obtain.

Fourth, students should be asked to locate as many sources that relate to their subject as possible, and to file them in the case folders. In some cases relevant sources will be found in books and periodicals that are part of the library's permanent collection. Since these sources cannot be mutilated for inclusion in the case folders, students should be asked to outline or summarize the article or book excerpt, and the outline or summary should be included in the folder.

Many commercially published casebooks include a list of possible research paper topics that could be developed from the material reprinted in the books, and teachers may want to ask their students to develop a similar list based on the contents of their case folders. The development of topic, or thesis, statements can be a valuable writing activity in itself, and such an assignment is one way to encourage students to read the material in the folders. A somewhat more elaborate activity along the same lines would require that students write several thesis statements and briefly outline the arguments they would use in developing each statement into a paper.

It should be noted that it is important to prevent case folders from becoming unmanageably large. There will be the temptation for students to include in the folders every piece of information they find on a subject, but to do so would detract from the value of the case folder. Students should be encouraged to be selective of what they include in a case folder, and they should be asked to evaluate the relevance and merit of each item in terms of what they learn about the subject through their research.

Case folders are certainly not the perfect solution to the problem of the research paper, but they can do a lot to eliminate some of the drudgery and pain research writing causes students. And teachers, too.

Getting Started with Fictional Biography

William Rakauskas
University of Scranton

A repeatedly successful technique for early-in-the-semester writing motivation is a procedure I have been using with my writing center classes at the University of Scranton. We go through a series of prewriting warm-up and review activities designed to provide sketchy content which students ultimately expand into a creative fictional narrative biography. The operation develops through four discernible stages.

In stage one, which lasts for two or three days depending upon class size, I spend the last fifteen minutes of each class session having members of the class present brief bits of information about themselves to the rest of the class. Routine though it may seem, this simple device does help to set an environment for the eventual composing sessions. I believe it is very important for the teacher to be actively involved, so I usually do the initial one as an example of what I expect the class to do. They are asked to give their first and last names, early education, place of birth, places lived, major hobby, interest, or sport, and reason for attending the University of Scranton. Often a very sure and confident individual really lets go, deluging us with idiosyncrasies. However, most offer a minimum biographical sketch. While each introduction is being given, the rest of us jot down notes.

After each person offers his or her sketch, the next person to speak must summarize some of what the previous student revealed. When the introductions are complete, I randomly select students to identify people in the class and to give one or two details about them from memory. Then I ask someone else to add to what was just said. By the end of this stage, there is not one student who is a stranger to the rest of the class. Equally significant, I know my students, not only by first name but also by what they were willing to reveal about themselves. Thus, a climate of support is established early. Students and teacher are now ready to enter stage two: inquiry.

During the inquiry stage, we spend one day reviewing principles of narration and clarifying a few necessary terms. I give no definitions; we search for clarification of principles and devices based on our past experience with narrative literature. I try to get the students to search their memories for examples of narrative devices such as foreshadowing and flashback from stories they have previously read. Gradually we establish some basic working definitions; for example, we agree that fundamentally narration answers the question, "What happens next?" We conclude that plot is basically a sequential connection of interrelated events containing a conflict and some kind of resolution. Permeating all of this is the fact that for narration to develop at all, an author must have something to work with, details from which he or she will carefully select and skillfully create a story.

Now we are ready for stage three — our own special kind of narrative, a fictional biography of the person sitting to our left. It is to be a brief, imaginative story about some aspect of the person's life. Arbitrarily, I set a three-page maximum, which forces the student to focus and expand on a few specific details. The class writes as much as possible in a period of twenty-five minutes; then they hold a cross commentary session for approximately twenty minutes. During this phase, I ask for volunteers to read what they have written. At first there is some hesitation, so I usually offer to read my first draft effort. This opens things up and soon most are in the spirit of the activity. I stress here that in no way can we expect a finished paper produced under these conditions. Our goal is to get something down on paper, to conquer the initial fear of the blank white page. Now that we have something down, and now that we have received some real audience reaction, we are ready to move to the next important stage, revision and rewriting.

Stage four takes place outside the writing laboratory. We allow ourselves three days to complete the final draft and to submit the final product for evaluation.

The results of the above technique have been genuinely satisfying. The students have fun and they do produce some clever papers. But most important, the students experience several important stages of the writing process and come to realize that composition involves prewriting, writing, and thorough revision.

Researching Old Murders: Creative Term Papers for Freshmen

W. Keith Kraus

Discarding the casebook in favor of old murders in the New York Times *made a lively research experience. W. Keith Kraus is assistant chairman of the English Department at Shippensburg State College, Shippensburg, Tennessee.*

Although a great debate persists over the content, methods, and even the concept of English 101 — including "revolutionary" articles advocating the overthrow of the whole thing — its companion course, English 102, fails to generate much excitement one way or the other. The most recent poll shows that a second term in freshman English is alive, if not well, in close to 80 per cent of colleges surveyed, and that the staple of the course seems to be the research paper.[1] Still, English 102, or what goes on there, fails to ignite violent passions, as does its predecessor. The impression one has is that teachers, if not completely satisfied with the traditional content of the course, are at least not dissatisfied enough to protest very vigorously. At least in English 102 there is real "material" to be covered, a real "paper" to be done. Footnoting must be explained, books located, literary works must be taught ("After all, I can't expect them to write a research paper on *Moby Dick* until we've gone over the novel!") — in short, there is a "hard core" of information to be imparted and there is no reason for that unspoken lament of English 101, viz., "What do I do in class?" So everybody's very busy — teaching, and researching, and reading *Moby Dick*.

I was looking under rocks for a better way to present the research paper and neither casebooks nor colleagues provided a lasting answer. Then a clue appeared. I devised a series of library exercises to acquaint students with general reference works such as *The New York Times Index, The Readers' Guide, Book Review Digest*, etc. Not that I planned to have my class use these sources in writing their papers really, but I found that most freshmen have rarely used any reference other than *The Readers' Guide*

---

[1] Thomas W. Wilcox, "The Study of Undergraduate English Programs: Some Preliminary Findings," *College English*, 29 (1968). See also, Ambrose Manning, "The Present Status of the Research Paper in Freshman English: A National Survey," *College Composition and Communication*, 12 (1961).

and have a deeply rooted fear of a college library. My goal was to give them practical exposure to standard indexes and reference materials, acquaint them with our library's rapidly expanding micro-resources, and I suspect, salve my guilt in the course by teaching skills which might be useful in further college work.

The first exercise directed students to look up the *New York Times* on the day they were born and write a brief paragraph about what happened. Standard enough. They learned to use the microfilm machines and maybe noticed we carry the *Times* back to its issue in 1851. Exercise two was designed to introduce the *Times Index* and the question was, "What were the circumstances surrounding the death of the following person?" And then each student was given a different name and date.

For years one of the fun books around our house has been a picture account of "the roaring twenties" which favors closeups of assorted gangsters riddled with bullets somewhere on Chicago's South Side. So for this question I lifted the obituary information on some of Capone's finest, put it on 3" x 5" cards (what else!) and dealt the cards out to the class, appropriately, face down.

When the assignments were turned in, a number of students mentioned how interesting the story was surrounding their case, how strange that era must have been, and in some cases how different the account read compared to a "modern" newspaper story. We spent a few minutes in class joking about some of the mores of the 1920 gangster world they had uncovered, e.g., gold coffins, funeral processions through the "territory," the man's rivals uttering B movie eulogies. It was obvious this had been fun ... for both of us. Looking up the review in *Book Review Digest* had been a chore, but the other was fun. Naturally, we forgot about all this when we turned to our "serious" project and everyone did his dull, badly done paper on *Moby Dick*. For the last time.

Before the next term began I spent a weekend in the library at the *Times Indexes* pulling out each volume, flipping to the "Murder" listings and noting the best cases dating from 1851. First, they had to be big enough to allow students to pick and choose from the available material, and to select from a mass of information the key elements, facts, details and quotations needed to construct a paper of about two thousand words. Second, I wanted cases that extended over a period of years in which new developments kept appearing and confusing the issue. This paper was going to be a legitimate test of a student's ability to research and organize scattered and chaotic materials. Third, I tried to pick cases that seemed to touch on some aspect of the American mind and character, that revealed a national or local attitude or strange custom of the time. For instance, one choice was the

1897 case of William Guldensuppe whose dismembered body was found over a course of three weeks, except for the head. His "remains," sans head, were put together and he was given an open casket funeral attended by thousands of curious viewers. Or, again falling back on the gangster crimes, I selected the 1929 shooting of Red Cassidy in the Hotsy-Totsy Club in New York. Simply from the entries in the *Index* one can sense the flavor of the period, of gangland rivalries, police corruption, missing witnesses turning up in the East River. Fourth, I picked only cases that looked interesting, somewhat bizzare, fun to read about and research . . . and to correct. No run-of-the-mill muggings, no domestic manslaughter cases, no same-day-confession crimes. I tried to find twenty-five "classics" — boy meets girl, boy accused of killing girl, boy released for lack of evidence, town lynches boy upon release, etc. But usually I had no idea how the crime turned out or really what it was all about, and no case was selected if it was so famous there were books about it (exit Leo Frank and Lizzie Borden). For all practical purposes this was to be "original" research, or as close as one could get in a second term freshman course.

From the outset I knew I had scored with my fourth objective. The kids were really fascinated with their projects, and although some of their cases were often as complicated as *Moby Dick*, few people had trouble "understanding" what was going on. The greatest difficulty was organizing the material and putting it into a readable format. I found almost everyone had situations where facts were misstated, jumbled, or conflicting. In cases before 1900 the newswriting style was as foreign to students as an article in a scholarly journal. Students constantly had to look up archaic terms and "sic" seemed to be needed in almost every quotation. At first some people felt snowed under with material until they realized the importance of the proper selection of information; but by degrees they began to realize that a story entitled "Police Continue Search for Killer" would offer little that was new and was hardly worth reading. (I was reminded of the typical comment I had heard on literary papers: "Every book says the same thing about *Moby Dick*, so what should I do?")

The papers themselves turned out to be the best I had ever received. They showed real hustle in the library and actual work in rewriting. A number of people found stories in papers other than the *Times* and a few people discovered magazine articles concerning their murders. A couple of students had referred to encyclopedias or history books for general background material. To the best of my knowledge no paper was plagiarized, a fact I attribute to the students' interest in their topics. There were no scissors and paste jobs, which may have been due to the built-in "narrative" structure and chronological progression of the cases. And most important of all, I enjoyed reading the papers ... even the single-spaced quotations over five lines.

Since then I have tried to refine and expand the project. Recent topics have dealt with famous political scandals, espionage cases, a biography of a minor historical figure, and treasure hunts. Some of the best papers have been on Indian "uprisings," in which students were amazed to read contemporary accounts of "gallant horse soldiers dispatching copper-colored wretches" (Ute Indian War — 1879) or how a group of Mormons used Indians to wipe out a wagon train of immigrants (Mountain Meadow Massacre — 1857). I now allow students to pick their own topics or "areas" if they wish and I have a few takers; however, famous crimes is still the most popular category.

I ask that papers be between seven and ten pages with a bibliography of at least twenty entries. I stress the use of quotations in the paper which are striking and I like conclusions that are evaluative or speculative. I tell students dealing with unsolved murders to construct solutions and some of these are so ingenious that I'm convinced that they've found the answer. But most important of all I know they've had fun working on the papers. Occasionally a student hits a dull case, but I make a note to drop it from my list after that. And, of course, not all papers have been successful. Like everyone else, I receive papers that need a good proof-reading or that lack continuity. A few people are unable to see the forest through the trees and spend pages recapping the predictable outcome of new trials and further appeals. I should add further that a few of my colleagues look upon this whole business as lacking in high moral seriousness, even though it has now become an official alternative in our freshman English syllabus. But this is a minor drawback.

For those interested in giving it a try I make this free, send no money or stamps, no salesman will call, boxtop-less offer. Send me a postcard in care of Shippensburg (PA) State College, 17257, and I'll mail back a list of 100 "uncontrolled" research topics guaranteed to interest students. These come ready to serve, just add the *New York Times* and the *Times Index* and distribute in your favorite class. Use them for four full weeks or so and if not completely satisfied, return the unused topics for a full apology. Order now and receive a bonus gift of a sample student paper reproduced on clear, easy-to-read blue ditto. (Offer void in departments where constricting rules prohibit innovation.) Never again be forced to read a freshman research paper that is pasted together from critical books, or culled from a single "work," or that is dull and predictable. Try to find a similar claim on the back of your *Moby Dick* casebook.